*special thanks to:*
Simone Suchet (Cultural Services, Canadian Embassy in Paris), Simone Urdl (Ego Film Arts), Alida Stevenson (Ontario Ministry of Culture Tourism and Recreation), Raed Skiri, Emmanuel Weber (Ecole d'architecture de Paris), Helen Thifault (Telefilm Canada), Corinne Collier, Félix Vincent (Imprimerie La Source d'Or).
Gaël Leroux, Bertrand David and Alban Barré (photographers)
as well as: Géraldine Bendayan, Marion Chopin, Patrick Lébedeff, Catherine Louveau.

Front cover: variation on a photography by Daniel Kieffer.

**Printed in France**

# ATOM EGOYAN

CAROLE DESBARATS

JACINTO LAGEIRA

DANIELE RIVIERE

PAUL VIRILIO

*Translated from the French by*

BRIAN HOLMES

This book was published with the support of the
Ontario Ministry of Culture, Tourism and Recreation.

THIS SERIES EDITED BY DANIELE RIVIERE

*In the same series*

PETER GREENAWAY
Daniel Caux
Michel Field
Florence de Mèredieu
Philippe Pilard
Michael Nyman

RAOUL RUIZ
Christine Buci-Glucksmann
Fabrice Revault D'Allonnes

MANOEL DE OLIVEIRA
Yann Lardeau
Philippe Tancelin
Jacques Parsi

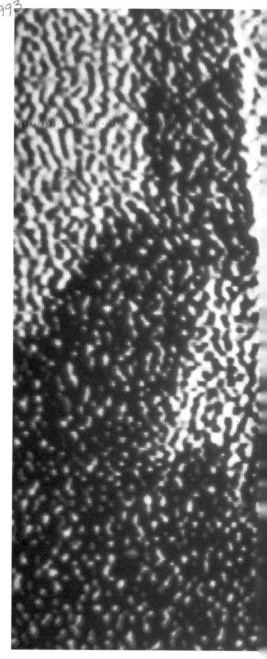

◄ 1

*I*n a world layered with images, the cinema of Atom Egoyan tries to single out the experience of the real. And yet this filmmaker is not interested in an arcadian authenticity, a reassuring excuse for a lack of hard thinking, integrity, and quality; rather, his quest accepts detours, meanders, skip-searches, the better to approach a reality that always slips away, but still can crystallize for the viewer in an instant of sensation or emotion. Atom Egoyan's movies show a world where two traditionally incompatible spheres are joined: the private intimacies of family life and sexuality, and the public access allowed by modern media technologies. ◄ 2

The force of these films is, precisely, that they don't give in to the fascination of a fumbling attempt to classify all the mediations that render direct experience so increasingly rare. Atom Egoyan subordinates his meticulous description of technological means to a world-view where man is apprehended in the dimension that cinema comes closest to: the body. Egoyan measures its resistance by the yardstick of film, focusing on the eroticized body as it is caught in the spotlight of domestic images, photographed, recorded for home-video, or on the contrary, confronted with the emotions sparked by TV broadcasts and various other screens: here, the bodies of good English-speaking Canadians subjected to the strange but somehow familiar flavors of Armenian food; there, the bodies of eastern women coming into contact with the pornographic images censored by puritanical Canadian society... This trial of the individual often blends with motifs offering a better grasp of the misunderstanding that separates and fascinates the sexes, or with figures of the confusion experienced by people from a different culture, a culture marked by genocide; but there are also portraits of a second generation, born of

Armenian parents but brought up on the new continent, young people who know that authenticity is never given but must always be won.

This larger framework is what makes Atom Egoyan's interest for the new domestic images into everyone's concern. He hasn't just taken a random sample: these slices of life compose a digital image bank, where a flip of the cursor gives us a report on the state of humanity, on the state of things in general.

Indeed, the images reproduced in his films offer the immense interest of being identifiable, placeable for everyone, at least for those in North America and Western Europe where video has seemingly been domesticated. We all know the danger of giving in to a major temptation, that of finding mediated experience more interesting, more true than our own; and sometimes we try to conjure this loss of reality by the appropriation of mass images through home channels. Perhaps this is what Atom Egoyan calls "the process of sanctifying the image" — in the face of which his intention is "to analyze the way these tools have affected and continue to affect our relationships with others and ourselves."[1]

Of course these last fifteen years, and particularly the eighties, are there to prove that the impact of the new images on the experience of reality is far from being the restricted province of Egoyan's films. This cinematographic inquiry is widely distributed, though with unequal success, across a spectrum running from the middle-of-the-road Soderbergh — who got the "palme d'or" at Cannes for *Sex, Lies, and Video Tape,* released the same year as *Speaking Parts* — to the far more disturbing Hanecke, the author of *Benny's Video*.

It is always difficult and sometimes even a bit ridiculous to try establishing the chronology of a trend. When it's a case of "household" sounds and images (as one says "household appliances"), the temptation shows itself to be vain: who began using surveillance images, for example? Chaplin with the screens of the director's office in *Modern Times*? Or Fritz Lang with his demon of evil and his *Thousand Eyes of Doctor Mabuse*? The fact is that the theme has been considerably developed, not so much in parallel with the evolution of video art as with the expansion of the domestic technologies market, and indeed of "household systems." No one will be surprised that North America and Canada in particular has provided an economically and ideologically propitious ground for the cinematographic treatment of this proliferating phenomenon. Among other examples we could cite a film that seems to have counted for Egoyan: *Videodrome,* from 1982. David Cronenberg uses modern communications gone amok as the fictional agents of terror, and to do so he works with the material of the film itself, inscribing it with different textures, marking various degrees of the construction of meaning and emotion.

If British-Canadian filmmakers have shown a particular interest for this theme, this can at least partially be explained by the very conditions of production governing the Toronto cinema of the eighties (dubbed, for convenience's sake, "the Ontario New Wave"), of which Atom Egoyan is a leading figure.

Canadian cinema in English and French alike is largely under the sway of the United States, those "southern neighbors" against whom northerners must defend themselves, as Atom Egoyan says.

Indeed, Canadian cinema suffers greatly from the mass distribution of U.S.-made movies in its territory, which is sometimes seen from down south as a simple extension of the internal American market. Is it in reaction to this imperialism, as Sylvain Granel suggests,[2] that Canadians have preferred to specialize in a type of film that doesn't poach on Hollywood's territory, privileging instead the documentary, the animated film, experimental cinema and new technologies, and showing a special predilection for the short? Whatever the explanation, Canadian filmmakers, from the two major language groups or from minority populations — Armenian, Ukrainian, or Hindi, for example — have taken over the old tactic that the Americans used to conquer the great prairie, occupying a territory disdained by the world-standard-setting U.S. films. In the context of this approach, the European model of *cinéma d'auteur* allows the Canadians to turn their backs on Hollywood and set out on their own. And in fact, alongside a Quebec-

based production which is more well known in Europe, English-speaking Canada is now ◄ 3 producing films whose importance has hardly yet been measured here in France.

Toronto, the city where Atom Egoyan works, is not only a major production center but also an intellectual hub, radiating out a number of film journals nourished by meetings between cineasts and screenings at the Festival of Festivals. The city was, in particular, the site of two emblematic events through which Canada declined its status as the "domestic market" of the United States, showing the world its own cinema. The first was the major retrospective organized by the Canadian Cinématheque in 1967, and the second, the two hundred films shown in 1984 at the Festival of Festivals, under the heading *Northern Lights*. This affirmation of the vitality of Canadian cinema, particularly in Ontario and Toronto, has been bolstered both by the recognition that cultural institutions such as the Cinématheque and the Festival can bring, and by the hard cash that certain financing organizations were able to offer, during the eighties, in support of projects manifesting an ambition to *cinéma d'auteur*. All this activity gave rise to the idea of an Ontario New Wave, partially linked, like its French predecessor, to certain ◄ 4 production methods; Atom Egoyan prefers to call it a new wave "of appreciation and recognition" for independent cinema from English Canada. It dates from 1987, with four low-budget productions: *A Winter Tan* by Maryse Holder, *I've Heard the Mermaids Singing* by Patricia Rozema, *Life Classes* by William D. MacGillivray, and *Family Viewing* by Atom Egoyan.

Of course these young filmmakers come together around concerns that go beyond the simple economic factor. For Geoff Pevere, "the staging of individual insignificance and powerlessness in so many films from Ontario and from Canada as a whole (in the eighties) stems from a skepticism toward the most fundamental principle of the Hollywood film: the belief in the transcendent power of the individual will."[3] Thus it's no surprise to find that various films from this decade give off the same feeling of "extreme individual and social disaffection,"[4] which resurfaces even in the locations chosen for the films, the half-empty homes of *Open House* and *The Adjuster* or the hotels of *Speaking Parts*. But Egoyan's work cannot be reduced to the key themes of the Toronto cineasts:

6 ▶

though his preoccupations may overlap some of the main lines of English-Canadian cinema, still they remain highly singular, very much his own.

His first shorts are marked by the influence of American and Canadian experimental cinema, that of Brakhage, of Snow.  In these works Egoyan seeks to exploit the different textures of the image, from video to silver emulsion, from documentary recording to animation, with a use of filters recalling the toning of silent films.  In short, the young cineast engages in an open-ended exploration of the image in movement, already practicing the method that will characterize his full-length works: putting the cinema to the test of other techniques.  In *Peep Show*, for example, he begins with a coin-op photo machine, registering and revealing sexual fantasy through a mechanism whereby film and money are combined.  With this third short, done in 1981, the main character is reduced to an auto-erotic voyeur trying to track down the sole proof of his material existence — his body — through the banal images of a public portrait-booth.

But experimental cinema concentrates on the visual above all, repressing narrative, which nonetheless interests our cineast.  Atom Egoyan is too fascinated by the "family romance" — or the "family film" — to give up telling stories; he just does it his way... Thus he likes to claim that in his films, the camera is a character.  This not only implies a layering of the narrative process such that the filming systems are not hidden from the viewer, but also an intervention of the camera in the story, and a treatment of viewpoint that is far more specific to fictional than to experimental cinema.

Thus an emblematic camera movement in *Peep Show* uses the autonomy conferred by fiction to take up Welles' system of "audience camera," an invitation for the spectator to follow the lens's point of view, detached from that of the characters: the narcissistic voyeur closes himself up in the private peep show of the photo-booth, and the camera, borrowing the famous opening movement of *Citizen Kane*, pulls us under the curtain into the booth, crossing the fragile "no trespassing zone" marked by the carefully pleated curtain behind which the "hero" gives free rein to his fantasies.[5]  Already in this

7 ▶

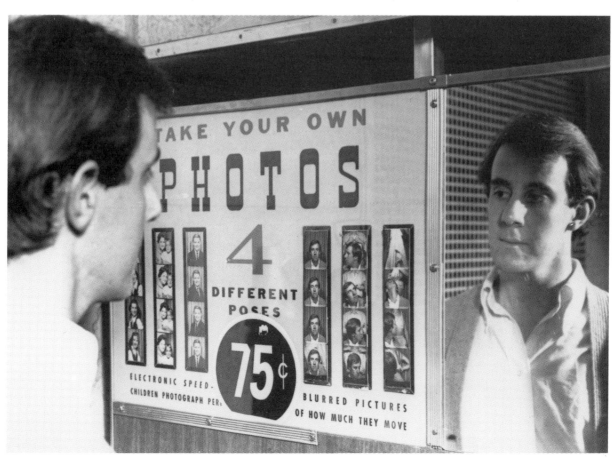

1981 short, it is sexually driven behavior toward the image that nourishes the narrative system. Obtaining no photos that satisfy him, the young man of *Peep Show* begins kicking the machine; a security guard comes to restrain him, and the camera "freezes" for a brief instant on his bound and gagged body, thus accrediting his existence by producing — in the juridical sense of the word — the momentary image of the petty news item whose hero he has become.

As an heir to experimental cinema, Atom Egoyan's system certainly displays its internal workings, but even more, it maintains the tradition of a film that meant a lot to him: Hitchcock's *Vertigo*. After the deconstruction, he proposes elements of reconstruction.

True to the spirit of the Ontario resistance, Atom Egoyan is also influenced by European filmmakers who deal in stories, but in a rather different way than their Hollywood counterparts. It comes as no surprise that his list of favorite directors includes Buñuel, Bresson, Resnais, and the Pasolini of *Theorem* — whom one recalls for *The Adjuster* — as well as Ingmar Bergman: all filmmakers of Evil, among those for whom the cinematographic art constitutes a reservoir of knowledge about human cruelty, but also, through an intimate correspondence, about the treasures of compassion. This marked interest doesn't function in the classic "film buff" way which linked the French New Wave to its forerunners: as a cineast starting off in the eighties, Atom Egoyan *also* has a familiarity with film through video.

Thus in an interview he describes his "primal" image, a shot from *Persona* seen at the age of seventeen or eighteen: "Confronted with the composition of this very strange shot where the faces of two actresses merge into one, I found myself up against a host of questions. How do people look at images? What do we expect from them? What do we see in them? For me, this type of cinema was very interesting and very new, because it didn't fit what we could see at the movie theaters. In fact it was on television, on a French channel we were getting here, that I saw *Persona* for the first time, which made it all the more fascinating to see that moment where Liv Ullman, who

◄ 8  ◄ 9

has lost her voice, sits all alone in a hospital room looking at a TV set broadcasting the image of a preacher."[6]  One can understand that the young man experienced, in his own terms, "a turning point" and "a crossover to cinema" with his discovery of these inter-locking images, from the unification of the double in Bergman's image (the two faces coming together in one) to the redoubled instance of the viewer (Liv Ullman and Egoyan himself), both linked together by the televisual substitute for the sacred.  Terrified of the roles imposed by their prosaic lives, the characters of this 1965 film finally come to exchange their personalities in what Bergman calls a "mirror scene."[7]

Atom Egoyan's filmmaking takes up these questions from the same starting point in the banality of life, with disaster experts, real-estate agents, housewives, dealers in Oriental trinkets, all of whom he subjects to the risks of video — conceived as mirror favoring anamorphosis over the impossible reproduction of objective reality.  And this very banality situates the originality of his cinema.  Rather than denouncing the dangers of specular proliferation in the fantastic vein of North American film — which tends to present video as a modern Pandora's box — or mustering up the resistance of a certain European cinema preoccupied with the power of the all-visual and the disappearance of meaning behind the polish of the images, Egoyan begins from a simple fact, the insistence of video images in contemporary life.  His films are therefore marked by the recurring presence of video technology, systematically treated in its different commercial or familial variants, from surveillance devices (whose diagonally plunging perspective he sometimes adopts for his own shots) to systems for recording family therapy sessions, then on to video-conference networks and funerary clips in a futurist mausoleum.  As we noted above, these are the kind of images that non-specialists can understand the best, right down to their mode of production: in their fabrication and consumption, they are the most common.

10 ▶

A sign of the times in the age of AIDS, some of Atom Egoyan's characters can only develop in a sterile milieu, under video light.  They live out their most intimate

◄ 11
experiences this way, like the couple in *Speaking Parts* masturbating in duplex: thanks to the simultaneous retransmission of their respective images by a video system, they are separated in space but present together on the same fantasmatic stage. In the shorts, the accent fell more on the different technical means for the reproduction of images and sounds, from the photo-booth of *Peep Show* to the tape-players, slide projectors, and answering machines of *Open House*; but with the first feature, *Next of Kin* in 1984, the interlace of video and intimacy is already manifest. For it is video that allows the main character to mix himself up with the family he has set his heart on: watching a tape destined for therapeutic use and which he has no right to be seeing, Peter (Patrick Tierney) conceives a violent desire to pick up where the psychoanalyst left off and help the family get back on track again. Thus he decides to take the place of the phantom, the missing son Bedros, whom the poverty-stricken Armenian family had given up for adoption. In *Family Viewing* (1987), the oedipal conflict centers around the domestic use of video recording, which is first devoted to the classic home video and then
13 ►
instrumentalized for the sexual needs of the father. In 1989, the narrative structure of *Speaking Parts* takes form around the video system, allowing the characters' desire to achieve a modern crystallization that no longer needs to wait for Stendhal's time-depth, but functions instead in closed loops, the same way Lisa (Arsinée Khanjian) and Clara (Gabrielle Rose) keep reviewing the recorded images of their fantasy object (Michael McManus). In fact, video is above all used to strip bare and thus to actually *see* the workings of what Atom Egoyan calls "the selective process of memory," best exemplified in the 1993 film *Calendar*. Here the filmmaker reveals the mechanism of an affectivity constructed from a back-and-forth movement between present and past, reality and fantasy; between lived experience in Toronto and the video images, which in this case are hardly indifferent, since they were garnered from Egoyan's first trip to Armenia.

In this last film more than ever, video is irreducible to a simple system for the
◄ 12
mediatization of the real. Of course it plays this role for some of Egoyan's characters;

but it holds another place in his films, where it serves as a narrative program in a certain way. In effect, the filmmaker nourishes his fictions by enumerating all of video's possibilities, as though inspired by the functions of a remote-control device: erase, speed-search backwards or forwards, and channel-hopping all become modes of being for the characters, who in this way find a cinematographic representation of their enthusiasms, their desires, their anxieties. In *Family Viewing*, the father erases the video tapes bearing the image of the mother to inscribe sexual scenarios with his second wife. In *Calendar*, the video image of Arsinée Khanjian in the classic pose of the tourist in front of Armenian churches comes back to haunt the photographer (played by Egoyan himself); the sudden acceleration of the reverse mode surprises the viewer, who initially thought he was seeing the character's present experience but now finds himself thrust into a fantasy-filled past by this new flashback technique.

In fact, what Atom Egoyan does is to test video's different possibilities as a narrative agent, somewhat as Godard makes use of all the means of film and video to impose the status of image onto text, his "regal enemy." Similarly, Egoyan varies his uses of these procedures: for example, he can make a more metaphorical employ of the reverse function, resurrecting the dead as in *Speaking Parts*.

Of this epiphany the doubling is born, no longer marked by a trick-table effect as in Bergman's film — with the fusion of two half-faces into a single, uncanny one — but rather by the simple cinematographic reproduction of the video image. Quite logically, this superimposition of images within the fiction entails the layering of the filmic narratives, and these multiple framings are matched in turn by visual multiplications of texture and grain: to regain access to a world buried in images, the hollowing-out of the narrative structure deliberately blocks the viewer's identification by a successive build-up of Chinese boxes, putting the brakes on a dramatic progression which is also deprived of the analytic resources of discursive language.

This refusal of a linear structure allows us to clarify the system brought into play by Egoyan's films: working with a classificatory procedure which is clearly being exploited for its libidinal value, the films carry out a denial of chaos that legitimates the characters' errancy.  The heros then project their egos[8] on each other, like the disaster expert in *The Adjuster* attributing his own state of shock to the victims.

Atom Egoyan's most interesting films are those where the order reigning in the fictional structure is put to the service of emotion and sensuality.  The world then begins to resemble the library of *The Adjuster*, a world in *trompe l'oeil*; and the artifice helps to brave the violence of a quest that can only find the real by submitting all that is most intimate, the flesh, the family, one's own language, to the test of the force that could take it definitively away, and of which video is only a privileged figure.

To communicate the experience of this disorientation, Atom Egoyan brings the viewer closer to what is being shown, but *simultaneously* pulls him away, subjecting us to a contrary movement that recalls the compensated follow shots of *Vertigo*.  In a world devoured by metastatic images, experience is at this price: one has to introduce elements that can help flake off the always-already-seen.  It makes you think about something Egoyan confided in a recent interview: "The first time I saw a body, I couldn't keep myself from thinking about images I'd already seen; there was nothing new in what I had just discovered."[9]

Blending intimacy and exhibitionism, domesticity and the openness of the public forum, Atom Egoyan lifts all protection from the private sphere — even more so because he denies his characters the recourse to language that would help keep chaos at a distance.  His heros have no faith in the operative virtues of discourse: "There is nothing special about words," explains Lisa (Arsinée Khanjian) to the man in the video shop of *Speaking Parts*, who is amazed to see her fascinated by a bit-actor appearing only in the background, and therefore necessarily silent.

The recent films push this experience yet further: one of the strongest characters in all these works, Seta (Rose Sarkisyan), the sister in *The Adjuster*, puts this defiance of language fiercely into practice — but compensates with representations of the flesh.  An

immigrant from the Middle East,[10] she refuses to speak English but gobbles up images of Canadian bodies, which her sister steals for her by pirating them with a video recorder during the censorship sessions in which she takes part.

◄ 14

In Egoyan's work, language is as intimate as the body and constitutes one of the major counter-investments against the visual proliferation described in the films. First of all because it appears on the soundtrack: in a representation where everything is too visible, the audible takes on a very strong value, above all at the level of an emotional perception which does not call for immediate analysis. Thus, again in *The Adjuster*, Egoyan confers their full violence on the pornographic *images* filched by Hera (Arsine Khanjian) precisely by not giving them to be *seen*, but only to be heard.

In his second-to-last film, *Calendar*, Atom Egoyan goes one step further by giving particular autonomy to the soundtrack's role in the ordering of the fantasmatic scene. In effect, to get the most out of his memories, the photographer (Atom Egoyan) needs a meticulous organization. Beautiful women bearing an increasing resemblance to his girlfriend make their successive appearances at his table, and invariably, at the end of the meal, go off in a corner with the telephone to talk to other men in an impassioned voice, and in languages sufficiently far-removed from each other to be largely incomprehensible for anyone but a true polyglot: German, Russian, Arabic, Greek, Hebrew, Spanish... These conversations are interlaced with sequences, themselves ritualized as well, of the couple's trip to Armenia, in the time before the image-maker's companion decided to chose the old country, thus forcing a break-up. The feminine speech of the strangers is sensual and incomprehensible, gaining the voluptuousness of music; the man always ends up alone at the table, in the remembrance of those moments when his Armenian-speaking girlfriend acted as intercessor between the country and himself, while he photographed or videoed it. At this point in the "selective process of memory," image and sound gather in the man's imagination, which the film shares with us: the voluble, laughing body of Arsinée is inscribed in the Armenian landscapes, alongside that of the man who guided them through this civilization, but who could not speak any English.

◄ 15

Thus in *Calendar* the multiplication comes into play not only in the video re-presentation integrated to the film, but also in the opacity that the foreign languages present on the soundtrack, for anyone who does not know them. The sequence where an Armenian-speaking man addresses the video recorder of the English-Canadian photographer constitutes the acme of the film. Atom Egoyan stages himself facing a man who speaks a language that is both familiar and strange, whereas during the dinners in Toronto he turns his back to the women busy on the telephone, thus reducing their speech to a simple sound environment. The Armenian speaks to the photographer as much through the *presence* of his body, through his wind-wrinkled face, as through his words. After all, there's nothing special about words... Hence the very moving scene where the passport is handed from one side of the camera to the other: a highly symbolic object which *connects* one body to another can also guarantee the link between two individuals separated by their cultures.

Ten years before, in *Next of Kin* — one of his most touching films, if not one of the most accomplished — the blond kid (Patrick Tierney), who has essentially become an Armenian by choosing an adoptive family, gives a speech whose failing is no doubt its excessive readability: "When you're raised with a group of people you're obliged to love, you don't ever really get a chance to see them as people outside of that group. And in a funny sort of way that means that... you can never really love your family, because you're deprived of the freedom that you need to make that kind of commitment; the freedom of choice." The Armenians present are involved in another of the celebration's rituals and so they don't listen too carefully, except two or three. Among them, a dark-haired young man, an extra without a speaking part, the filmmaker himself.

Atom Egoyan knows Armenian rather poorly and cannot read it: "I speak it a little because it was my mother's language, but less than before because I don't get much practice. Anyway, I like this idea that you lose one language to gain another. It re-appears several times in my films."[11] Indeed, his childhood was marked by a great concern for assimilation, followed by a self-willed effort to rediscover his culture. The

**30** ▶ cinematographic testimony to this is the importance he attaches to all sorts of family rituals, and indeed to sexual rituals as well: they allow for the establishment of anchor points, of shelters, which some characters find in video, others in elective affinities, others in the family or in the intimate theater of their sexuality.

Nonetheless, Atom Egoyan does not voluntarily strike the posture of filmmaker of the Armenian diaspora. Instead, he works with his Canadian/Anglo-Saxon culture, measuring it by what Armenia brings him; he does not immediately espouse the Armenian heritage, but rather progressively makes it his own. One recalls what the Armenian father (Berge Fazilan) says in *Next of Kin*: "When you start with nothing, every bit you earn fills you with pride. It is yours."

**17** ▶**19** ▶ In fact, the temptation of Armenia is shown in his films as the slow search for a present, and this quest is carried out by putting the individual, the family, and sexuality to the test of everything that can cut through the stereotypes and help get closer to authentic experience. The approach isn't surprising, coming from a man forged in the school of filmmakers like Buñuel and Pasolini, who envisaged human beings through their sexuality or through the specific kinds of knowledge preserved in popular culture, or Resnais and Bergman, who were fascinated by mental and emotional mechanisms, or the experimental filmmakers, who worked with the material of the image to try out new visual forms.

**18** ▶ Now Atom Egoyan sails ahead with the speed built up over a decade, pursuing in his films an expertise on the state of things and of beings. But what could be no more than speculative experience is weighed down with heavy emotional ballast: the consciousness of the world that comes from an acceptance of the "fundamental tumult" described by Bataille. Whatever the means used to send Evil back home for a confrontation with the characters — the multiplication of reality's reflections, the dynamic engendered by the clash of cultures and of languages, or still other modes yet to come — the principle of Atom Egoyan's cinema remains the same: conquering what they tell us is "natural," and making it truly one's own.

*A*mongst the plethora of public and private images dispensed by the cinema, the television, and the video cassette player, everyone has had the chance to experience the gap between the memory networks constituted by the simple recording of events and the memory we actually have of these events. Our recollection of words, gestures, places, and actions only rarely matches the sequences and image-structures fixed once and for all by the machine, without any possible alteration (lest it be in the very materials used for recording). But not only does technical memorization replace the factuality of beings and things when we seek confirmation of our own remembrance in a second look at certain images; even more, this technical recall actually becomes a new part of our memories. When we see a fictional film or a domestic video tape, the recollection of our accumulated memories appears as a second or third layer, superimposed and inserted in sequences which, in the long run, seem to belong neither to the image nor to its initial trace. And though the "sequence" forms part of the cinema's plastic grammar, it bears a very close resemblance to memory as well: not just since the latter also emerges by fragments and not in totality, but above all because the sequence in images can itself induce new memories, in the same way that our memories continually and paradoxically engender unique moments.

◄ 20

The characters in *Next of Kin*, *Family Viewing, Speaking Parts*, and *Calendar* have at least this much in common, that when they turn to the past, they only search for memories fixed in images — avid as they are for mechanically recorded eras, voices, gazes, and bodies. They speak very little about their own memories, as if wanting to repress them, or to hide the impossibility of saying them outright; vision takes over for individual or group rememoration, and sometimes comes to overdetermine verbal exchange. Charged with revelations and inevitable deformations, the *projection of memory* in an act of anamnesis often seems to replace real memory. Atom Egoyan's films unfold in this way, by images referring to one another, legitimizing each other, contributing their reciprocal testimony to gradually reconstruct the puzzle of memory. It is only by fitting the parts one into the other that the overall image takes shape, for the remarkable thing — also suggesting a puzzle — is that each part is already a little image, a little memory. Each sequence is related to the others, even while developing its own structure, its own world. But although mechanical recording is related to a memory circuit objectified by the distancing inherent to the machine in use (camera, video device), still the agent or victim of the stored-up images struggles to keep memory alive through his or her choices, despite the power of memorization. This power stems from the objective part of the machine, which presents recordings allowing for generic recognition by any viewer (inside or outside the film/the story), whereas true memory belongs only to the actor-viewer. Being a singular moment of human experience, whether secret or shared, memory is the final rampart against the depersonalization carried out by machines and the media. But it is the most fragile as well, for the terrible effort involved — collecting diverse references to places, persons, and situations, in the hope of fabricating a memory — often veers dangerously toward the absurd: it is not certain that a whole can be attained, since even this whole will then become another isolated part.

*Public/Private* Some of these scattered parts find their place in an ironical dialectic between private and public, which functions in a circular way, but without any final resolution, since it is always seeking to establish the identity of the two opposing poles. Like the majority of the characters, we watch television with our families, we replay images that we have filmed (meals, marriages, vacations), we rent or buy movies — in short, our behaviors are the same. But the apparent identity of these everyday activities soon turns around against us, because we are doing precisely what the film describes:

watching a film. Thus slippages take place between character, actor, and viewer, through multiple variations inside a closed system. The characters can become the voluntary or involuntary "actors" of a film shot by a third person with a video camera, while still remaining the actors of the film watched by the spectator on the movie screen or a home TV set; the spectator, outside the film, can watch certain scenes filmed in such a way that he seems to take part in them, just as he can identify with the character, who is also a spectator when he watches a cassette within the film. The person looking at the image, wherever and whoever he is, must be able to take on the two roles simultaneously for his curse to be fulfilled.

Watching *Family Viewing,* we see a young man, Van, watching cassettes filmed by his father for very private use, since they record sexual scenes with the father's second wife. This isn't only the classic abyssal structure of "story within a story" or "film within a film," but above all the institution of a perverse relation between private and public, between spectator and actor, all the more so because the cassettes in question hold information that can be destined either for the public or the private sphere. Indeed, these same tapes contain unerased sections showing family scenes between the father, Van as a child, his mother, and his maternal grandmother; in these cassettes, the characters of the films become public "actors," but also private ones, in their relationship to themselves. Although the images are private, such simple memories can nonetheless be presented to people outside the family circle, whereas the erotic scenes are reserved strictly for the amorous interludes of the father and step-mother. It is not a matter of different degrees, but of diverging points of view. The father has combined sequences which from his viewpoint are *all* equally private, but which from his son's viewpoint are either private *or* public.

The visual limits concerning what is permitted and what can be seen are difficult to determine for the young man in *Family Viewing,* as for him these limits remain inseparable from affective boundaries. It is quite obvious that the step-mother indulges the father's sexual fantasies in order to stay at home with the young man, on whom she showers both maternal and amorous effusions. She redoubles the confusion between

22 ▶

21 ▶ 23 ▶

24 ▶

private and public by superimposing filial love (emotional outpourings in front of the husband-father) and heterosexual attraction (which is kept scrupulously hidden from the husband-father). Her attitude borders on incest: despite the non-genetic family ties, the ban is still there. Chancing on the cassettes with the erotic sequences, the young man simultaneously discovers childhood scenes in the company of his grandmother and his mother, also filmed by his father — images which he doesn't seem to have seen since the actual event. Thus memory, recollection, love, sexuality, and parental law are all inextricably linked through vision; and they become emotionally linked as well, since they remind the young man of an entire range of sleeping life-experiences which seem never to have been articulated in his exchanges with his father or his step-mother. The only person who could have told him scraps of history about his mother and his childhood is his grandmother Armen, who is the *incarnation* of recollection and memory — and not just the vision or the image — but who can no longer transmit anything verbally. All that remains of the past are the father's cassettes; and so the son brings these same cassettes to the hospital, after having first selected only the family sequences, in order to project them for his grandmother. She is reassured, happy, seeing her daughter and her grandson. Even though she is in a room with several other patients, the young man judges from his viewpoint that these private images can be shown before all. Thus they become public images by the will of the grandson, but also because there is only one television in the room. And yet if these images, now become a publicly exhibited memory, remain nonetheless an intimate possession for the grandmother and her grandson, still they are not just meaningful for these two alone. The cassette's viewing public (the other characters) are also able to recognize themselves in these generic family images, just as the exterior spectator can easily integrate his own life-experience into the family schema: the public spectator can then become a private actor, and the public actor, a private viewing public.

In Egoyan's work, and this holds for numerous films, certain private sequences can become public without being altered, while others lose their credibility when shown to a wider audience. The latter case applies to the images that replace memory and an emotional bond for the young man in his difficult relationship to his father. These are images which were recorded at a time when the family was together (or supposed to be at least), but which were then destroyed by others: they are sequences belonging to the father's private sphere, but encroaching partially on the son's. The young man continues to have a relative attachment to his father, so long as he doesn't *see* certain things, so long as he doesn't discover certain secrets through the intermediary of the paternal cassettes, concerning moments in which he was inscribed without knowing it. He has never understood — and could never possibly have understood, for lack of explanations — why his grandmother hates his father. The answer is supplied by a cassette he has not seen and which he inadvertently shows to the grandmother: amidst the family scenes there suddenly appears a sequence from an earlier recording, presenting his mother on her knees, bound and gagged, her gaze turned imploringly toward the camera. The truth is out: the father forced his mother to submit to his sexual eccentricities. Thus the young man is a witness, years later, to what could be identified as the "primal scene." It is a private scene, the solution to the enigma of the child's origins, revealed in images which could traumatize an individual's identity; but it is also one of the constituents of his personality in social relationships. A private structure thus becomes operative in the public sphere.

The memory of the events captured by the cassettes allows the characters to read their own memories differently, to clear them up, to sharpen them, indeed, to *create* them purely and simply. The flashbacks to the past throw new light on the present, for the characters as well as the spectator. The indifference or hate between the father and his mother-in-law begins to look like a mirror reflection of the love between grand-mother and grandson, while the affection between the young man and his stepmother is the negative image of the terrible relationship between the father and the maternal grandmother. The point of origin for the memories of these three characters is precisely the absent image of the young man's mother, which had already appeared in other forms, *beneath other images* memorized by the father for his personal use. When he saw them for the first time, the young man did not suspect that these later images were

**25** ▶ the delay-broadcast *repetition* of what had already happened with his own mother. He had seen shocking things played out between his father and his step-mother (who, by the way, was quite familiar with these video images of a mother whose son would become the object of a love denied to his father); but this was only another version, another recording, of what he could have stumbled on between his real mother and his father. He was already present at the moment when this private image was fixed, but at the time he only moved within the circle of the public images that his parents chose to show. He needed a certain number of scattered images, of dispersed memories — and several years in the dark — before the missing parts of the puzzle would all come together. Once in place, not only does his present life change, but also his present remembrance, because the discovery of one part of his memory causes him to recompose an entirely new image of the rest. So these are not only fragments of the past that he finds through the machine's memorizing system: he also *sees* a previously unknown memory, transmitted by the image and not by his life experience. Machine memorization now becomes the deadly memory of a living being, imprinting its indelible seal on his mind.

*Substitution/Identity* The spheres of public and private function in tandem with other parameters: they are essentially mirrored by structures of substitution and identity. The story of Peter in *Next of Kin* is that of a physical substitution, but also of a mental one, carried out in the attempt to recreate or simply create an identity. After visually stealing certain images destined for the private use of a psychotherapist in a clinic he visits with his parents, Peter has the idea of taking over the place of another, of playing a role before false parents and all their relatives, that is to say, in public. Thus he merely concretizes the feeling he has always had, of being divided in two, of being both audience and actor. He becomes clearly conscious of this while watching himself in the company of his parents, on a cassette recorded by the therapist during an interview. Not only does Peter-turned-Bedros take the place of another young man, thus creating

**26** ▶ patterns of family relations, or rather, filling in the empty framework of these relations,

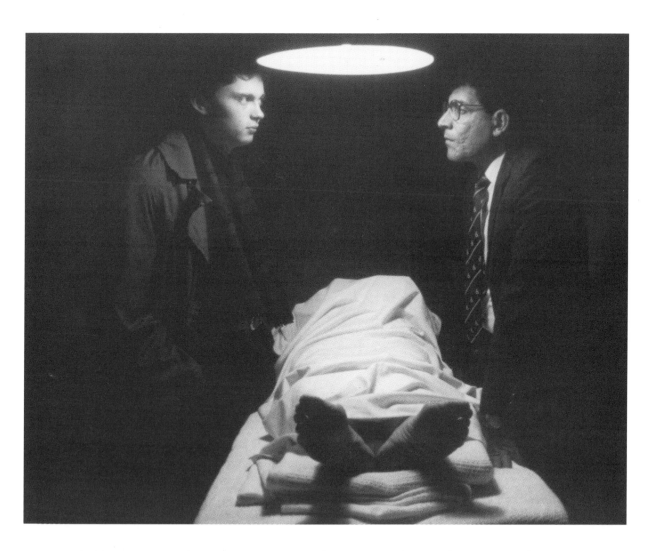

and so restoring an identity to his true-false family — what is more, he invents an
identity for himself.  And the substitution here lies not so much in passing himself off for
another as in the fact that without even knowing it, he replaces his new family's identity
for another one, made up from scraps.  Because in fact, this family identity, *rediscovered*
as if by a miracle, actually never existed.  It is Peter's invention, but it is also an
unconscious identification by the family, replacing what they have always longed to
recover: a son and brother, given up for adoption while he was still a child.  The
memories are therefore fictive all around, but according to the different viewpoints they
are either perceived as a reconstitution of the self (Peter), or a recomposition of the
family nucleus (the father, mother, and sister).  The temporal paradox of this encounter
resides in the fact that Peter seeks a kind of future escape-route to what he was unable
to obtain in his childhood and adolescent relationship with his parents, whereas the
family wants to fulfill in the present what was frankly impossible in the past.  Indeed, by
comparison to the borrowed family Peter has the advantage of having memories
concerning his past, even if disagreeable ones, whereas the family has neither memories
nor future: their only wish and possibility is to actualize an imaginary being, here and
now.  Peter is alone in his knowledge that he plays the two roles and that his only
reason for joining this family is to better rediscover his own identity and return to a
more normal relationship with his real parents.  But in Egoyan's world, these types of
moral and emotional substitutions are only possible, or are most *successful* and *effective,*
when the bodies themselves can be exchanged.

In *Family Viewing*, the young man takes advantage of a girl who has asked him to
watch over her mother while she goes on a trip: when the old woman dies, he switches
her over to the neighboring bed of his grandmother, to make his father believe that his
grandmother has passed away.  It is no simple act of vengeance for the young man,
because he, in search of his mother, substitutes the body of *another mother* for that of
his grandmother.  Thus it is paradoxically *someone else's mother,* the mother of a girl
with whom he could trade places to recover mother/child relations, whose
disappearance he brings about.  Again in *Family Viewing,* one of the father's fantasies

consists in filming himself in bed with his second wife, and asking her to perform on his body the caresses that another woman whom he does not know dictates over the telephone. At this point, only the couple in the bedroom know they are being filmed. They hear the young woman speak without her knowing that they are not only listening to her, but also watching themselves in an image that is directly retransmitted on television. Thus the father's companion incarnates the voice and replaces the absent body of the woman who speaks unwittingly through the machine. Finally, in a scabrous retrospective irony fueled by the memory of previously seen images, the young man's step-mother becomes the active body of a present voice which doesn't belong to her, while his grandmother represents the nonexistent voice of an immobile body. The young man can now see his step-mother, and above all his grandmother, as substitutes for his absent mother, either through sexuality and perversion, or through sickness and death: the four structural elements of a narrative which Van's mother is the only one to knit together, symbolically or in reality.

In *Speaking Parts* we meet a sister who tries to recover the image of her brother, suddenly deceased on the operating table. To gather her memories and free herself of them all at once, Clara writes an autobiographical screenplay for television, then enters by chance into a relations with a young actor who bears a strong resemblance to her dead brother. The coincidence becomes even more astonishing after she films him for an audition. Here, the recorded and rebroadcast image is not an obstacle between past and present; on the contrary, it confirms the past by unfolding in the present. Thus the videographic images — of the past or the present — act to free the sister from a part of her anxieties, while at the same time inscribing her not in the register of immediate reality but rather in a perpetually mediated existence. It is no doubt for this reason that the two characters, who become lovers, communicate so frequently through closed-circuit video. For Clara, the past continues in this video present, all the more so because she herself had filmed her brother shortly before his death and now replays *in private* these few images that remain to her. By speaking to the young actor through a video system, she is able to commune with her brother. The actor, Lance — who only knows her brother through the fixed image of a photograph — quite consciously takes his place, because this substitution allows him to play a first television role. Thus he acts out a fiction, while becoming a real actor in relation to the woman; but he also actualizes her incestuous fantasies about her dead brother. It is through the body of the actor-double that she is able to claim her brother's body and accomplish the reprehensible act (as we infer by suggestion, even if no real sexual act is shown); but in this way she simultaneously redeems herself and relieves her guilt for his death, for which, we later learn, she was partially if unwittingly responsible. In effect, the brother's surgical operation was supposed to save her from a disease through the donation of certain organs, and therefore through a physical substitution, another form of body reversal. The body of the young double gives life to the irretrievably lost body of the brother.

*Next of Kin* also deals with the physical absence of the son's body, an absence relived by the mother when she explains to Bedros her regret at not having been able to hold him longer in her arms when he was a child; Peter lends himself to the game, curls up like a baby and lets the mother cuddle as she will. The absence of the lost body is thus compensated by the present, rediscovered one. Even though the contact between mother and son is physical here — rather than taking place through images — it is nonetheless partially a feint, a falsehood, and partially a new and living reality issuing forth from this very duplicity. The role-playing thus comes to create an element of this family's memory, and the original fiction transforms itself little by little into a "normal" life. The photograph of Janus-faced Peter, inserted into the album, will attest to his presence and his place within the configuration of the family.

*Family Romance* The films present a fundamental characteristic that returns in diverse scenes and sequences as one of the numerous models of recollection and memory. It is easily recognized as "the family romance." The structure described by Freud (the inventor of the notion and the term) applies very well to the case of Peter in *Next of Kin*. Dissatisfied with his family, neither recognized nor loved by his parents, he goes off searching for a substitute that can bring him (or so he hopes) the affection he is lacking. But contrary to the Freudian description, where the behavior of family-romance neurotics consists essentially in fantasy activity, Peter passes to the act with the help of subterfuges that come directly from the psychotherapy session he watched by chance, *just after* viewing one of the sessions in which he participated with his own parents. This "acting out," which at first seems quite unlikely, is closely linked to the manipulation of the cassette containing information about the family, and to the fact that over the same television, with the same recording devices, and in the same room, an absolutely *identical* interview occurred, leading to an *identification* on Peter's part, thanks to the images alone. They offer a mirror image of his family situation, complete with identities and reversals. As in his own home, the parents (and above all the father) do not *recognize* their daughter; the young woman is Peter's age, but she represents the *opposite* sex; and to cap it off, this family is seeking a son who really *exists*, while Peter is looking for a family that only exists *in his imagination*. By staging these complementary fantasies, Egoyan evokes the power of the televisual image much more than the power of reality and desire. Before looking on as the viewer of absolutely private family scenes, Peter had already maintained that he was alternately actor and viewing public in his own family and that he could *watch himself* acting the role of son before his parents. Indeed, when he finds his true-false parents, Bedros carries out the consecrated gestures of the son by kissing them; but so doing, he imitates the behaviors of the therapist, seen earlier on the tape. He identifies with the therapist while also replacing him, since by becoming the son this couple was longing for, he also provides the most effective therapy: love that heals all wounds. When he saw the cassette, the substitution took place in and by the image. All that remained was to give it a body.

*The Adjuster* also partakes of the neurotic family romance and perhaps to an even greater degree, given that sexuality is very much at issue here, along with a kind of fantasmatic pornography that functions by allegation from one character onto the next.

30 ▶ One of the conscious attitudes of the adolescent or the adult in the family romance is that when he feels shut out by his parents or loved ones, he *invents* extra-conjugal sexual relationships in order to legitimize his actions. (It is because he has swiftly imagined just such a relationship that Peter reproaches his false-father during the scene with the cabaret dancer in *Next of Kin).* In *The Adjuster*, it seems as though the family nucleus has enlarged, taking in ever more members. The insurance agent Noah and his wife Hera (a pair of premonitory names) have no sexual relations, even though her work consists in censoring pornographic films; during the screenings in the company of her colleagues, she uses a video camera to secretly record the films so she can replay them for her sister Seta, who lives with her. Neither of the two sisters has any sexual relations, but instead they realize their fantasies through the pornographic films, becoming the spectators of deeds they would like to act out. With this difference: the *actors* of the films make role and action coincide, whereas Hera and Seta legitimize their attitude through an imaginary identification with the characters. Becoming characters in their turn, they avoid physical contact — which would be the materialization of what the image shows them — and also compensate for their refusal of the sexual act. As to the insurance man in *The Adjuster*, he goes outside his own family to carry out his conjugal duty (if it can be so called). He gives moral support to his insurees, comforts them, devotes all his energy to helping them, becomes their friend, their confident, and most often the lover of the women. Thus he steps in for the husband (when there is one) or for the lover (when there isn't), taking someone else's place within a fictive couple or family and holding the role he can't play at his own hearth. He also passes to the act and doesn't rest content with simple scopic pleasures. Unlike his wife and her sister he is an actor, not a spectator: but it is through his very action that he rejoins the "family romance," since he does nothing but *fulfill* what the two women see in their films (as he knows full well, but hides from them). Doubly an actor, he perversely savors this situation, since he is both behind the curtains and out on the stage. But perhaps his 31 ▶ wife would like to use the films she brings home as an intermediary, to spark off in her

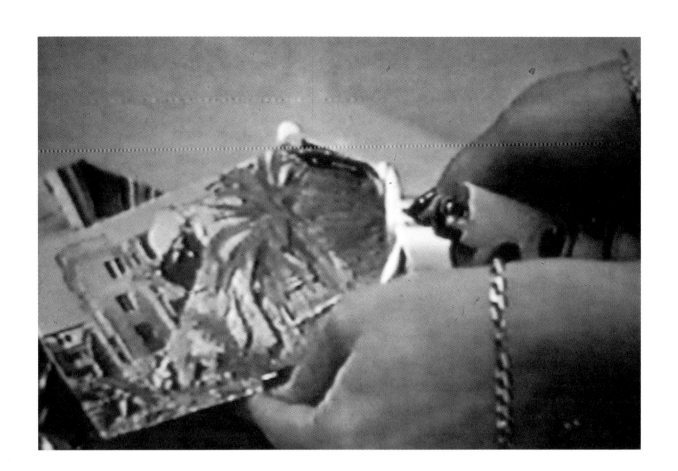

sister the same love that she denies her husband: one sister can easily substitute for the other, since they participate in the same family circulation of erotic images, some of which remain imaginary while others are realized.

*Substitution/Transformation/Narrative* One of the points Freud stresses with respect to the "family romance" is the constant desire for fiction on the part of he or she who plays the hero, the leading *actor*. It is easy to see that this desire to invent stories, to imagine fictions, is preponderant in Egoyan's films. The more fascinating thing is how the characters like to transform the narrative during the film, as if the actor had stepped out to become a viewer, altering the course of a story that he can't accept as determined in advance, as definitive and irrecoverable. The characters intervene before machine memorization stops all action, as long as their own memories still function — because memory always goes beyond the reasonable, rational limits of simple memorization, of simple technical recording. Thus in *Family Viewing* the young man, Van, spirits away his father's erotico-familial cassettes and replaces them with others, changing the labels, while the step-mother watches (and says nothing to her husband). He does it, of course, to show the tapes to his grandmother and see himself as a child again in his mother's arms, but above all to force his father into changing the course of the story in which he knows he is implicated, and which is being willfully kept secret from him. It is also in order to influence the course of a story still foreign to him — and not out of compassion — that he asks his father to visit his mother-in-law. Van's intervention in the parallel narratives of these two characters is not in vain, since a violent reaction from the grandmother towards the father confirms the existence of a hidden story. And it is once again the *will to know* what has been concocted behind his back while he was a child that leads Van to trick his father into believing his grandmother Armen is dead: he wants to push the father into wrongdoing by intervening in his personal narrative. Paradoxically, the family story in the video scenes of *Family Viewing* is almost mute, the words having been replaced by images which fabricate and engender a story that is hidden from Van, but which is also *his story*. The young man stages characters like a

◄ 32 ◄ 33

cineast stages actors in the attempt to have them *replay* his already written tale; thus Van, manipulating bodies and scraps of information, wants the others to play out the secret drama of his own existence, as if he were outside the characters' world, the attentive viewer of a theatrical fiction.

In *Speaking Parts,* the character who finally changes the script is no longer someone implicated in a story where he hopes to find his identity, his place, his raison d'être, but instead is an authoritarian producer, a veritable TV potentate, who is completely exterior to the scriptwriter's autobiographical leanings and simply plays his true role. Like Hera, the wife of the insurance agent who makes her living by censoring films, the producer also censors the films that pass through his hands. Both represent the pre-public, a still restricted viewing public working within the "semi-private sphere" that precedes public space. For the public's greater pleasure or, more precisely, for what he imagines as the public's greater pleasure, the producer transforms the script without notifying the author (who finds out too late). Thus this true-life story is falsified, deformed, but also *recreated*. The producer leads his viewing public to believe that the show — concerning the ethical problems of organ donation — is being broadcast live, whereas in fact everything is acted, prepared, staged. The actors and the extras who play the public and the participants of the debate recreate reality by transforming the original story: it becomes a common event, a talk show. Even though it is at the limits of fiction, of the simulacrum, of the unreal, the broadcast is nonetheless believable. The private life of the scriptwriter will therefore not be transmitted as is to the public, because the producer knows by experience that "fiction is even stranger than truth." In this way the producer intervenes in the parallel story developing between Clara and Lance, since his alterations, which Lance tries to make him give up for love of the author, will be the indirect cause of the relationship's end. Lance prefers to become a true actor, mediatized and public, rather than being a private actor, the substitute brother for the scriptwriter.

Similarly, in *Next of Kin*, it does not suffice for Peter to physically take the place of Bedros; he also has to invent his character, to find a story for him, to fabricate a fiction so as not to awaken the suspicions of his true-false parents. But this time it is not only the substitution and transmission of televisual or videographic information, of screenplays and therefore of *written fictions*, that will change the course of the rediscovered family's story; rather it is the corporeal presence of Bedros, the lost son who returns in flesh and blood. The substitution of the body takes place to allow for the creation of the character and the fiction that Peter will play out before his public (just as an actor is said to *incarnate* a character). The story can unfold quite smoothly, given that the fiction *really exists* in the eyes of the true-false parents, instead of existing potentially in an image or a text, in a near future or a distant past. The image of memory has become flesh, for a part of this family's memory has found *its narrative materialized as a body*.

It is in quite another manner that the insurance agent of *The Adjuster* composes his character and succeeds in transforming his own narrative. By doing with his clients what he can't do at home, he creates a second life, completing or filling in the gaps of the first and forming a parallel narrative that never intersects his family story, except through the pornographic images filmed by his wife. Films of this type include a minimal plot, just a pretext for the real scenes, the real actors, the *real film*: the sexual act. In this respect, the professional life of the adjuster bears a strange resemblance to the structure of the pornographic films. The scenes where he comes to the rescue of his female clients — comforting them and quite literally bringing them a little human warmth, indeed getting into bed with them — could easily be porno clips. He goes even farther in the reversal of bodies and roles, since a relationship with one of his male clients makes the sexual inversion complete. This parallel story is kept hidden from the eyes of his wife and her sister, but in fact they watch it unfold day by day in their films: they see it, but without knowing it. Contrary to *Family Viewing* or *Next of Kin*, where the characters' parallel lives are revealed by the image, the act of looking here draws an even tighter veil over what really exists. The truth remains outside the image, because it is only too present. Continually absorbed in the unfurling images, the two sisters submit to the theater of life and its countless representations, but they withdraw from the experience and knowledge of their lives by the same token. Vision is not always insight.

*Marked Places/Anonymous Locations The Adjuster* presents the quintessence of yet **34** ▶ another type of memory developed in Egoyan's fiction, another one of the scattered parts: the dwelling place. These locales are sometimes anonymous, sometimes marked by specific persons and memories. The scenes that keep the adjuster alive —both financially and emotionally — unfold in sites that are foreign to him. No adultery takes place in the family dwelling; it always occurs in anonymous locations, in this case the hotel where he lodges his clients until they find a new home. But on closer consideration of his "parallel narrative," these seemingly anonymous places — neither the family dwelling nor that of his client — are actually temporary meeting spots from which a certain degree of anonymity gradually fades away. Since the encounters take place quite regularly in the same hotel room, the place sheds its anonymity and becomes more marked, almost familiar. The adjuster's relations with the client are no longer professional but intimate, they are no longer public but private: in this way, the trysting place is transformed into a *second home* that fits right into his parallel existence. Since it is in a certain sense the unhappiness of his clients that makes his good fortune as an adjuster, and the despair of female clients that provides him with sexual gratification, he becomes their temporary shelter, their moral refuge. But because he does not respect the contract that consists in insuring his clients rather than abusing them (albeit with their consent), his actions are finally punished through the destruction of what is for him the most useful and fundamental thing of all: his own home. For this home is a fake that reflects the gestures and deeds of the characters: it is the simulacrum of a home, just as the adjuster's family, his relationship with his wife, and his sexual life are all facades to better hide reality.

Noah's home symbolizes and contains his entire existence: because he is an actor, he needs a stage decor. An extraordinarily rich woman obtains from him — through the intermediary of her factotum (or husband?), who passes himself off as a filmmaker — the permission to rent his house for a few days' shooting, because she requires *this house alone*. And so the adjuster, who spends his time negotiating contracts against all possible kinds of damage to other people's homes, will finally see his own home go up **35** ▶

37 ▶

in smoke, after a fit of madness descends on the supposed "filmmaker." But a premonition of the destructive power with which the adjuster is invested had already come in the form of his regular archery practice against the immense billboard outside his back window (a publicity picture of a model home, complete with a model family). Perhaps this baleful force is at the root of all the film's accidents: when Seta burns pictures of dwelling places, her act could be a mirror image of the esoteric magic that sets fire to houses from a distance. Thus, in this logic of the blind curse, the conflagration staged by the pseudo-filmmaker had to be lit in *this house alone,* as an application of a rather Kafkaesque law whereby the insurer who committed adultery from one apartment to the next, who often left his home at midnight on rescue missions to others' dwellings, could only be punished by the destruction of the foundation of his entire existence. Yet it is not a matter of moral condemnation, of guilt or expiation — these would be reassuring explanations — but rather of the simple unfolding of a simulacrum, in all its fallacies, distortions, illusions, and lies.

◀ 36

The absurd masquerade of *The Adjuster* recalls Van playing the film director to undo family traumas, because here a filmmaker (or more precisely, a character playing the role of filmmaker) finally arrives on the scene to shoot an erotically tinged film in the very home of the adjuster. It isn't exactly the same type of film, though a scene between the half-naked rich woman and a group of children suggests a certain dose of perversity and voyeurism; still it's comical enough to see the shooting of a true-false film precipitate the adjuster's fall. Rather than real images (like the cassettes that Van watched and the clips consumed by the two sisters), this is now a reality being filmed: a film *inside* the house. A metaphorical transformation finally turns the characters' play of parallel roles and narratives and the actors' exaggerated gambits in the porno films into a monstrous and devouring reality. An anonymous woman and a pseudo-filmmaker arrive to take over a private home which has no personal value for them, exploding the narrative of the place and its occupants so that, bizarrely, a similar narrative can begin all over again. The house, a site of false memories, must be destroyed to make room for

38 ▶

another house and its story. The fire certainly appears as a purification, but one could

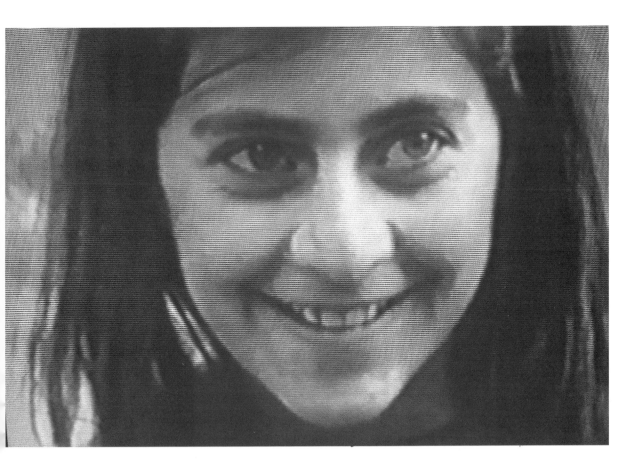

also understand the flames as the fulfillment of the simulacrum. The *real film* is wrapped up when the shooting of the *fake film* literally obliterates the house, and it is because the film inside the film destroys the dwelling place that *The Adjuster* can begin again, replaying its point of origin at its conclusion.

It is in another anonymous location, again a hotel, that Lance of *Speaking Parts* chances on the photo of a young man he does not know, alongside a screenplay that will allow him to affirm his identity as an actor. It is in this anonymous dwelling that encounters take place between Lance and his female clients, with the encouragement of the hotel director — the bodies circulate anew, offering themselves, identifying with other bodies and other fantasies — while at the same time Lance struggles to escape the amorous advances of a co-worker. Van of *Family Viewing* will also have recourse to the hotel where he works when he seeks to hide his grandmother, and it is here that his father attempts to erase the last of the traces that incriminate him. Whether it be for erotic, familial, professional, amicable, amorous, or personal reasons, the hotel is the anonymous location for all passages: here it is easier to go from public to private than the reverse, unlike the marked place represented by the family home, where the private takes precedence over the public. If the family dwelling is a highly significant place where most of the scenes of hate, intersubjectivity, and solitude take place, this is because it is so deeply marked by memory. Domestic video recorders and cassettes have the function of maintaining the memory of each individual who has contributed to family life, as well as the memory of the house as the preeminent place of origins, since it is frequently here that the traumas and the psychodramas take hold, that the neuroses break out. It is within the family dwelling that the pathologies originate. The hotel is an anonymous location where certain unforgettable events can unfold, but contrary to the family dwelling, the hotel does not contribute to the *formation* of an individual's identity, even if it may reveal key psychological traits. Through their remote-camera systems, the hotels simply memorize passing people, they record an ephemeral presence. The private detective hired by Van's father to discover what his son might be up to is, in his person and his actions, the very example of anonymity: in an anonymous location, he films people anonymous to him, with a machine that does no more than technically record the events. For him these images have no meaning, they just further depersonalize the beings they record. Thus the anonymous location can only produce anonymous images, sequences whose only consistency derives from mere memorization — except in the case of the videographic recording of the psychotherapy session in *Next of Kin*, where the spatio-temporal displacement of the family image, recorded and reviewed in the clinic, *visually reveals* Peter's role playing and dramatically confirms the fact that he is no more than his own double. Here the neutrality of the location seems to be a guarantee for Peter's act, as though the welcoming topography of the clinic were the space of a passage from one identity to the other, from one time to another, since Peter is moving from a memory to be erased toward memories to be created. The clinic or the hospital are places on the border between public and private, between the anonymous and the individuated. This is what allows Van to interchange the bodies of the two patients, to manipulate the data and trick the hospital director, or allows Peter to appropriate the identity and feelings of another family. Because of their nature, these places are both marked and anonymous: they receive singular beings, each with his or her own personal history, but all of whom are there for similar reasons linked to organic or mental pathologies. The very function of these places is ambiguous, to the extent that they reconstruct the corporeality and the identity of the individual at the same time as they render all these bodies and spirits homogeneous, dispossessing them of all that makes them unique. Beyond the total indifference that Van's father shows for his mother-in-law, it is no doubt for this reason that he heads to the wrong bed and believes he sees Armen, who greets him, finally reconciled. All these sick old women look the same; he no longer recognizes her. In this ambivalent location, the individual becomes anonymous, the other is no longer recognized as a singular being, but simply as the Other. Here, the father who had once filmed his mother-in-law in the garden now no longer recognizes her, and in the absence of memory he has not even retained a simple memorization. He is not even a machine capable of recording the image of a face.

39 ▶

40 ▶

*Self/Other* The experience of self and other must also be apprehended according to the placement, or staging, of several elements. The most immediate experience of the self is, of course, that of one's own image reflected in the mirror. The heroes come across mirrors in the bathroom or bedroom, as if symbolizing the need to find themselves as they really are — or perhaps just as they see themselves, which finally comes down to the same thing since they only identify through an immediately reflected image. In the contrary case of an image of the self retransmitted on closed-circuit television or replayed after a more or less recent interview, a gap creeps in to distance the image, since it is mediatized, temporalized, just as its spatialization can be magnified or reduced by the screen. What such an image foregrounds is essentially the narcissism of the beholder, a rapport to the self that very often passes through sexuality. In *Family Viewing*, the father desires to see himself again after the sexual act, while his wife, who faces the television, sees herself both during and after; and in a scene from *Speaking Parts*, Lance and the scriptwriter have a purely sexual relationship through the two televisions that reciprocally transmit their images, the narcissism here becoming fully auto-erotic. The viewers are also the voyeurs of their own spectacle, the public of their own act. They plunge into the death instinct linked to narcissism. Those whom they see on the screen are indeed themselves, but distorted, modified, captured by the machine: they become beings reified by a mechanical gaze, which replaces their own vision, itself now inhuman. By the intermediary of retransmission systems Van's stepmother becomes a sex object for his father, while Lance is no more than an imaginary receptacle for his script-writing lover. Whether actor or spectator, character of the film or character in the film, fiction or reality, they are finally no more than things. And when people are no more than things, it is because the recognition of self by self no longer works, nor the recognition of other by other. Thus the father of *Family Viewing* no longer recognizes his mother-in-law as a person, but as a thing on the way to death, an other who has rejoined the world of objects.

◄ 41 42 ►

However, not recognizing others can also be a benefit. In *Next of Kin*, Peter can fit better into his true-false family because the other he incarnates cannot be recognized, neither physically nor psychologically. And this non-recognition of the son who was thought to be lost forever is what later allows the father to recognize his daughter, by the intermediary of her supposed "brother," as though an identification always had to work through a third person, as though one were obliged to substitute the pieces of memory to recognize one's own flesh and blood through a stranger (which is what Bedros really is). For Bedros is finally the Other, and the fictive son is an Other thanks to whom the veritable daughter can come back into the bosom of the family. When the father falls victim to a heart attack, the mother and the daughter both hold him in their arms and at the father's request (which seems like his *last* request) Bedros takes a picture of the three: it is the stranger, the foreigner, the one outside the viewfinder, who produces the image of the family reunion. And this image can only be created if the Other is outside. This sequence recalls the scene in *Speaking Parts* when the scriptwriter joins her brother on the screen and they are filmed by an Other situated off-camera, an Other who could be identified with the Machine.

*Calendar* is a multi-faceted mirror where the Other multiplies and shatters into fragments. First by the obstacle of language, since the *narrator* needs an interpreter to translate what the guide is telling him. This narrator, whose body is never entirely seen and whose face is completely absent from the screen during the Armenian sequences, is thus foreign to the film; but in return, the people that come under his camera are also seen as foreign by him. When the guide plays the KGB agent and demands the cameraman's passport, the identity card attesting to his outsider status, he examines it as though it were the Foreigner in general. The image reflects this by placing the narrator off-camera, even though he is the one filming the scene. The guide is also the Other as rival, the one who seeks to steal the narrator's girlfriend. Indeed, he seems to fulfill certain conditions making him a reference point for the girlfriend's memory; in him, she rediscovers a part of her identity. And yet this Other who incarnates the memories of the girl is in the same blow the one who steals the amorous memories of the cameraman. Situated between the lives of the cameraman and his companion, the person of the guide crystallizes the same and the other, stranger and friend, a moment of identification and of rejection.

The images of self and other can also complete each other while remaining separate, as in the scene of televisual masturbation in *Speaking Parts*, where it is the action alone that makes the bond and permits the empathy; or again, in the many scenes where Lance's co-worker replays the cassettes featuring her sweetheart as an extra, cassettes that offer her the chance for fusion with the image whose reality she so ardently desires. Sometimes, but quite rarely, the fusion can go deeper: when the scriptwriter watches the images of her brother, doesn't she see a little something of herself in this vanished being? She *recognizes* herself in him — and this, even more so because she carries some of his organs inside her. It can also happen that the images of the self and the other fuse completely. In a short and very beautiful sequence of *Calendar* the guide steps behind the narrator while he is filming his shadow on a wall, and the two shadows merge to the point where one can't tell which parts belong to which body. At this point the film freezes on the image, as if to explain that the other is not only oneself perceived as an image, but always-already oneself *as the image of another*. In Egoyan's films recognition is therefore always double: both the *material* recognition of an image, a person, a place, and a *mental* recognition which is nothing other than the recognition of the content of an image (and this is real memory). To the first mode corresponds a genre of images resembling those which Lance sees of himself, of his audition: the image of himself as actor, replayed on the small television placed atop the table. Here we again encounter this permanent oscillation between spectator and actor (cf. *Next of Kin)* since Lance is the other seeing himself playing a character with whom, like any actor, he must identify; but he is also someone taking on the role of a real person (the brother) whom he must replace. His acting is double, because by playing out the sister's fantasies (reality) he also plays out a script (fiction) written by this same sister. He incarnates memorization and memory, but neither constitutes his individuality: in

43 ▶

◄ 44

both cases he remains an actor who, in the last instance, is the victim of his own theatricality, of his own act. The Other is therefore not only the brother he is in the midst of playing, but also himself as his own double. To the second mode correspond images linked directly to the experience of the spectator, lived memories, as in the case of the grandmother in *Family Viewing*. Armen is a pure gaze that loses itself in contemplation of the happy days with the family, in the vision of herself as she was, and in the vision of her double: her daughter.

Recognizing oneself as another is one of the recurring themes in Egoyan's films. The most striking sequences concerning this thematic are found in *Family Viewing*, when Van (re)discovers himself as a child in the family garden. The video tapes show familiar places, people, and objects: the house, the garden, the grandmother, the mother, the father, his playthings... but who is this child playing on the grass? Van seems to have some difficulty recognizing himself, or perhaps one should say that he does not recognize himself because these images are quite simply unknown to him. No sign in the film tells the viewer whether Van remembers these scenes, and everything proceeds as though the images did not belong to him at all. He has gone from being an actor to being his own spectator, but without recognizing himself — that is, without recognizing himself outside the categories of "actor" and "spectator." The memorization of space and time by the camera disfigures the familial environment, the place of identity, the site of intimate constitution for Van who sees himself on another stage playing his own role: the role of the Other. This other who plays and sings on the screen, these marked places which are the garden and the family dwelling, these perfectly identifiable people, all assuredly form part of his memory — but since when? Does he blend these memories with already existing ones that they only reinforce, or do these images immediately become new memories? Are they memories taken *from* childhood or applied *to* childhood? In the second case, it is again a third person, the grandmother, who confirms the authenticity of the images and assures the young man of their accuracy with her gaze. With her experience, with her personal memories, the

◄ 45

grandmother protects the young man from what might otherwise be a remodelling and repersonalization of memory by the image.

*Repetitions/Mirrors* It is no accident that the grandmother of *Family Viewing* becomes the mirror of Van's memories; since she neither speaks nor writes, it is in her gaze that the young man must find the confirmation of his actions. He sees himself in her eyes, both in the past and in the present: this is the maternal gaze, replaced here by Armen's (who repeats the gaze of her daughter). Of course, Egoyan's work continually suggests parallels with the gestures and words of our daily life (or the lives of others, which reflect our own image), but beyond that, the repetition and mirroring effects are also another way of forming or deforming memory. This is the case for the "primal scene" of *Family Viewing* which is *repeated* even as it takes place for the first time. But the *repetition* first happens with a substitute figure (the step-mother) before it is seen with the mother, in a kind of fantasized memory from childhood which resurfaces into the life of the young man. All throughout Egoyan's work, a multitude of sequences play off each other within the same film, either through simple repetitions of situations, actions, and words, or by mirror effects between the images. In *Family Viewing* the same words are reused in similar situations by different characters; Lance's young co-worker in *Speaking Parts* constantly replays the same films where Lance appears as an extra; in *The Adjuster* the fires, the seductions, the pornographic films return cyclically; in *Calendar* the same scene reoccurs ten times at the same moment with the narrator, etc. Mirror effects are no less common: the scene between the therapist and the family in *Next of Kin* and its successful repetition by Peter; the self-image in the television as the deferred reflection of the self in *Speaking Parts*; the false film within *The Adjuster* that contains and alters the opening of the real film (whose cyclic interlinkages could otherwise stand for the allegory of Repetition in general). Paradoxically, repetitions are what unfold normally, without really deforming the events that have already taken place, whereas the mirror images usually give rise to distortions, deformations, and simulacra. But very often repetition rejoins reflection, making it difficult to distinguish them. In *Next of Kin,*

46 ▶

the scene with the young thief in the store run by George, Bedros's false-father — a scene that the "son" watches attentively, as though seeing himself under the paternal reprimand while still a child (seeing oneself in the Other) — will be repeated again in a parodic way when Bedros, disguised, pretends to steal from the false-father's garment display. In the same way, the scene where the "filmmaker" sets fire to the adjuster's house merely repeats and reflects the numerous fires that have ravaged the houses of his clients. The mirror image can therefore be both a physical reality and a simple theatric device; but most of the time, the effect is more meaningful than the primary reality. This type of sequence is almost always turned around backwards and finally bears more resemblance to a counterfeit or a transformation of reality than to its reflection. The narrative by images and in images which was foreseen at first is radicalized along the way, becoming the simulacrum of itself; the characters no longer live in reality but in the images of reality, and this is what allows for all the possible and even imaginable permutations between homes and hotels, for the substitution of bodies, places, and stories, for the vertiginous whirlwind of identifications, fantasies, and role playing, for the madness of sexuality, perversion, and voyeurism, for the loss of self and of the other, and the disappearance of all memory, finally culminating in the scattering of the simulacrum itself. In *The Adjuster*, is it not to put a stop to the simulacrum — his own and that of the other characters — that the "filmmaker" sets fire to the house while choosing to remain inside it himself? His death is what halts the simulation. Let's remark in passing that the play of mirrors and of repetitions can unfold from one film to the other, since the filmmaker's self-immolation can be seen as a reflection of the scriptwriter's suicide; not only do both these characters write stories, but they both die for the same reason: to put a halt to simulation. It is also to call a stop to their suffering and to finish the simulacrum of life that the grandmother's ward-mate in *Family Viewing* commits suicide with an overdose of medicine, and a hotel guest in *Speaking Parts* finishes herself off in her room. In this continual composition/decomposition of repetition and mirror reflection, everything is marked by the failure of sexuality, of filial love, of friendship, of the family. All is rendered absurd by sickness, death, violence, pornography, the Law, censorship, madness, and childhood trauma, by the infinite and morbidly schizophrenic play of roles and functions. Nothing comes to its conclusion, nothing makes any sense, unless it is the simulacrum of a meaning or a finality — and this even holds for the memories whose recollection into a whole seems to be the driving force of the story, but whose very existence and reality eventually starts to tremble and fade away. For the simulacrum created by these images traps those who seek to escape, and, at a certain point, the specular narrative is less a transformation than a desperate run before the storm, onward towards the absurd: when Van rediscovers his memory thanks to the tapes, isn't he following the father in his tricks and manipulations, despite their very different aims? And isn't he therefore marked with the paternal Law that he seems to simply repeat?

*The Memory-Screen* A single schema — with, of course, a host of modulations — seems to apply to the composition and reading of the five feature-length films. It includes the central and recurrent thematics of the Family, the Home, and the Self, with which the puzzle can be put together. They obey the two principles of *direct* and *indirect* memory, with this bipartition operating throughout most of the works and ramifying in an involuting manner: the characters and images almost always return to a point of origin situated in the past. If one reconstructs the puzzle on the basis of this schema, some very curious formations begin to appear. In the case of the direct memories, the characters have already had experience with what they see again in the images, and the video systems that serve the anamnesis are present in the films like living beings: one feels them acting like persons, like participants in the scene. The camera becomes a subject, and memory coincides very often with the memory of the device. Such is the case in *Family Viewing*, where the memories of the family members are one with the recordings situated in Van's childhood; or again in *Speaking Parts*, where the scriptwriter possesses images and memories of her brother, and even physical traces in the form of transplanted organs. In the case of the indirect memories,

47 ▶

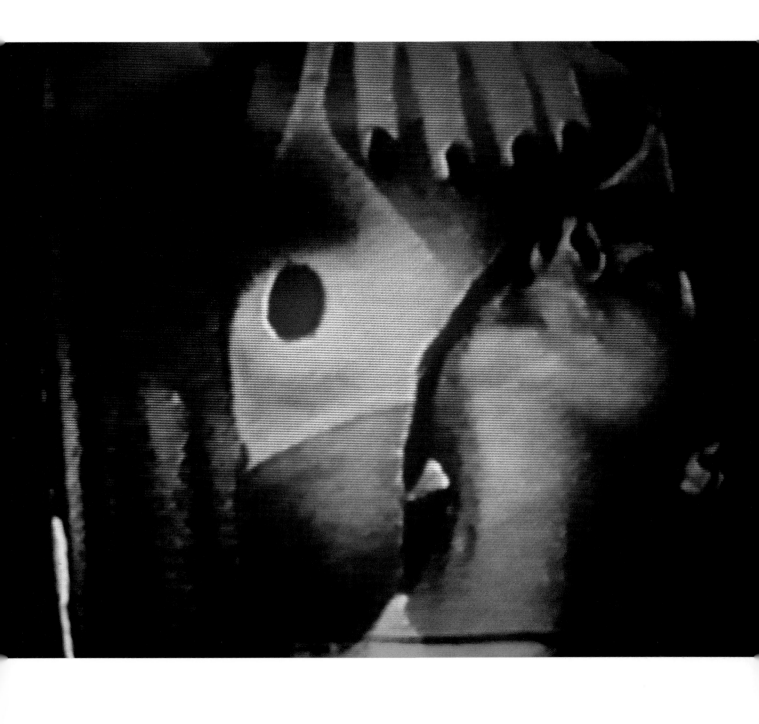

we are generally dealing with people who are caught in an intense identity crisis, but seem to have no real memory to hang on to. In *Next of Kin* and *The Adjuster* in particular, the characters live in an imaginary world peopled by their fantasies alone; they dream an identity, a way of life, people to love — and find themselves faced in the end with their own narcissism. In such situations the camera is, so to speak, *absent:* it has a memory that can be consulted, but no life experience links the spectator to the image. The great difference between these two aspects of memory (the one lived, the other invented) lies essentially in that for the first case, memory necessarily precedes the process of memorization by the recording device. For the characters who have actually lived the scenes and images that they watch, the machine never physically or materially replaces the bodies and memories; whereas for those who literally invent their memories, plucking them from the imaginary and not the real, the electronic memory is what creates the memory of the viewer, replacing his own power of recall. The first have to reassemble the pieces of an already existing puzzle in order to create their memory, where the second group have to fabricate the pieces they are putting together. But both are caught in the same trap: *memory must become image.*

The fact that memory must take the form of the image to be projected on the screen is fundamental. Watching Egoyan's films repeat this existentially vertiginous structure to the point of nausea, the viewer has the terrible impression that something ontological has been uncovered here. As though there could be no memory without an image to gather it, safeguard it, memorize it. For this is a non-living inscription, the mechanistic prolongation of a simple tool which becomes a physical and mental prosthesis made up of a screen where memory springs forth: a crutch that has become more important than its user. Contrary to the human being, the machine does not deform, does not imagine, does not rave; it does nothing but present the material inscription of what has been filmed, and the spectators or actors of the sequences are the ones who can see that as memory. And yet without images there are no memories; without fantasies, no life. Through the absurdity of this interdependence one understands that Egoyan's fictions are not attempts to reconstruct the puzzle but on the contrary machines to fabricate the shattering and scattering of its parts. In reality, the characters find a purpose for their existence in their diverse searches for the pieces, because without the initial shattering their lives would be yet more insufferable and alienating. The projection of memory onto the screen, in as many pieces as there are sequences, is similar to a prior harmony where each piece of the puzzle contains and reflects all the others. Beyond the immediacy with which they act these memories out, beyond the fantasies, the forgetting, the hate, these characters want to leave the incoherent world in which they live and retreat toward the prior harmony, where structure replaces chaos. By continually reprojecting their direct or indirect memories, either in images or in their imagination, the characters want to escape their real death, and their symbolic death as well.

Real memory or the fiction of the family romance allows them to momentarily find themselves in a role, in a function, in an identity where the image which completes and organizes itself little by little tends to be superior to the entropy that disorganizes and splits them. The image of death can be organic or physical disease, madness, the disappearance of bodies, fire, the reification of persons, morbid sexuality, voyeurism, or the weight of family life: and this image is all the stronger when its parts are more scattered. The characters' stubborn attempt to reconstitute the puzzle, to line up the images, stems from the fear of an infinite expansion of all the pieces. Here is the essence of the absurdity: they do not feel alive until they seek to recollect, but they can only act if some degree of dissemination pre-exists their quest. By filming scenes of their daily life to keep them "in memory," they seem to keep a part of the reality, an image of the presence of things and beings they can't really save (that is, keep alive). The paradox is that the recollection process seems to be stronger than the memories themselves, just as it seems stronger than death. The characters of Atom Egoyan's films would all be at home in a sequence from novelist Paul Auster's *City of Glass,* where a character named Peter Stillman says to another character passing himself off as his son, also named Peter Stillman: "Memory is a great blessing, Peter. The next best thing to death."

*O*ne of the "background images" at work in Atom Egoyan's cinema may be fire, as it appears in *The Adjuster*. Fire, the power of the gods' master, stolen from him by Prometheus (the "fore-seeing" one) to the greater good of men, but also to their misfortune, since they will be condemned to the redoubtable trap with which Zeus would punish them: woman, the "fair evil" from which none succeed in escaping, the beautiful Pandora with her jar containing hope and all the ills of the earth. Fire is both a vestige of the primordial invention of mankind and the focal point of an imaginary register of materials, an archeology of technical knowledge whose symbolism, rooted in socio-cultural traditions, can also provide a metaphor for Atom Egoyan's films. His is a cinema that stages the ritual of our everyday acts through the private images that we produce of ourselves, photos and videos which diffract the perverse effects of other images from the films of the times, Canadian in this case, marked by a documentary tradition (but now seeing the screens fill up with "cute little animals"[1]) and ◄ 51 stamped as well with the puritanism of Hollywood-style cinema, mystified and antiseptic. Held back on the screen is a body "whose erotic soul has flown,"[2] leaving only our images to unfold the intimate poverty of beings in dereliction, walled up in their silence: voyeurs of a unnameable body, their senses riveted to their communication machines or to the recorders of their fantasies.

*Of Gods and Images*: The blazing homes and charred photos of *The Adjuster* testify to the presence of fire, as does the Noah/Hera couple, with its implicit link to Zeus. For if the character Noah, gathering errant, free-floating beings in his motel, can make us believe in the emblematic figure of Noah and his ark — what with the ambient feeling of a recurrent "deluge" — still one can't fail to remark that women have taken the place of animals, and fire that of the flood. This is a first false lead. Nonetheless, through this very rough translation pierces another, more recognizable image, when the Biblical representation of the Deluge is compared with the Mesopotamian myth that makes Noah into humanity's first wine grower. In this initial moment of the deconstruction of the image, however, the filiation of Noah from his Biblical homonym barely trembles. The Mesopotamian avenue could seem to be another false lead, if the reference to the vine did not also evoke the wine of Dionysos.[3] This second stratum of the image permits an association with Dionysos on his boat returning from Egypt (the land of Atom Egoyan's birth), from whence he brought the grapevine: a representation which seems to have been inspired by the same source as the legend of Noah. And here, alongside Dionysos, we begin to see the profile of his antithetical double, Apollo the archer, suggested by Noah at various points in the film. Apollo is both the protector of order and justice, and the death-dealing divinity who propagates the plague. Apollo and Dionysos, the gods of the arts, and the figures of two antagonistic understandings: for one conceives art as the reality of the dream, and the other, as ecstatic intoxication, a dreamed reality.

These would seem to be the archetypes articulated by the filmic couple, Noah and Hera. Noah would be only a stage in the metamorphosis of Dionysos, himself twinned with Apollo, both illegitimate sons of the lightning-god Zeus, and both obliged throughout their lives to hide from the view of Hera, Zeus's legitimate wife, whose wrath they flee, pursued for the crime of birth. In *The Adjuster*, Noah has become the expert in fire insurance, while Hera, whose original role was the protection of legitimate unions, has been entrusted with the control of images.[4]

But in this context, what can be the value of a contract established with a man who is supposed to protect, to insure, to guarantee the everlasting security of lifestyles — if his identity is uncertain? If Noah is someone else? And what credibility can be accorded to the perspicacity of the censor of images — when she hasn't even been able to see that the other whom she dogs unflaggingly, furiously, whom she pursues to the far ends of the earth, is actually living right beside her?

*Of Gods and Men*: Woven through this filiation of mythological and legendary figures, between historical time and fundamental time, between chronicle and narrative, is the web wherein the recurring themes of Atom Egoyan's cinema intertwine; where the gods, subject to the laws of succession and the dramas of conflict, fall into the body and thus into the redoubtable trap laid by Zeus.

This passage from cosmogony to anthropogony illuminates the function of ambivalence at work in all of Egoyan's films, which involves localizing the moment — between "de-structuring" and "re-creation" — that inaugurates the current conditioning of human beings. The myth of the Deluge evoked in *The Adjuster* and the associated symbolics of fire stand in this respect as a doubling of the origin, situating humanity today at the issue of the original catastrophe whose liberating action figures a re-commencement: "all that begins in this world is the beginning of a world, a re-creation, but in return, all creation can stand for that which began only once."[5]

The "family resemblance" between the Biblical and the latter-day Noah therefore translates as the resurgence of a time situated between decrepitude of one world and the advent of a new one, in which the mythic story of individuals and of their successive incarnations is to be told. This return of memory transposed from the level of cosmogony to that of eschatology no longer operates as the quest for origins but as a means to reach the end of a time, to put a limit on the cycle of generation and repetition. The gamut of "trials and punishments" — which in the traditional description of the myths of memory was reserved for Hades (Hell) — is now applied to terrestrial life, which in its turn has become a world of oblivion. Here, the "waters of Lethe" are no longer associated with death, but with the return to life, with existence chained to the wheel of fatality and birth, which effaces "the memory of the world and of the celestial realities to which the soul is related, among those returning to the earth for a new incarnation."[6]

52 ▶

Thus the couple of Apollo/Dionysos reunited in one body is glimpsed in the figure of Noah, where he who binds, Apollo, finds himself attached to Dionysos, expressing the plasticity of time that characterizes Egoyan's films. This is an art of time as dream *and*

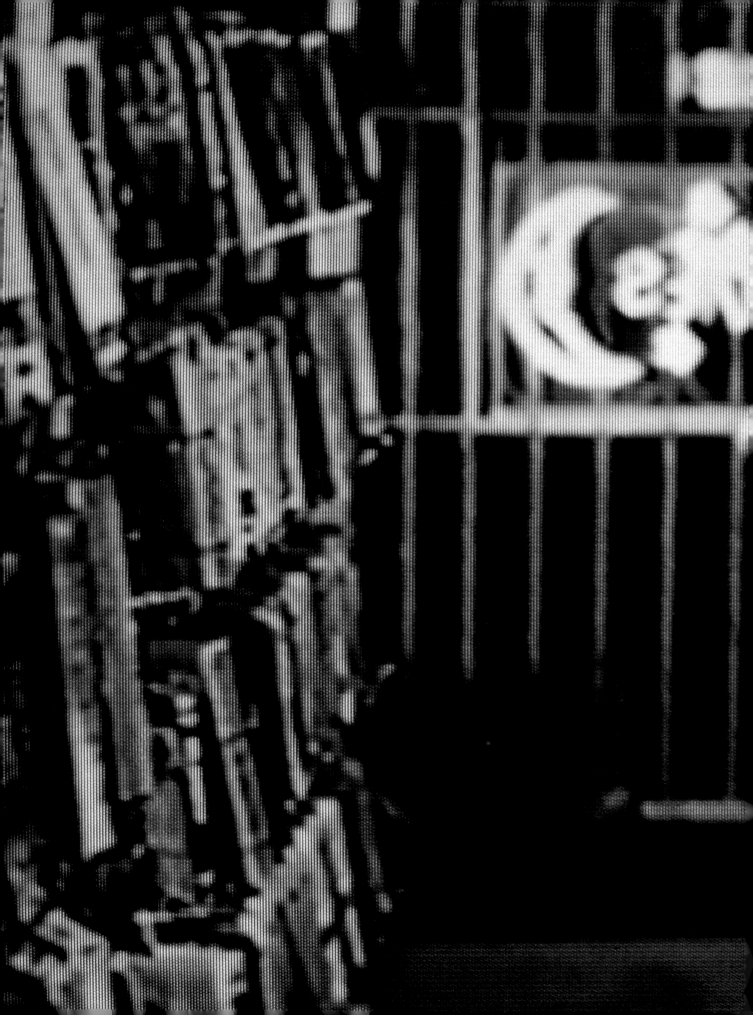

intoxication, a "dream state" which is no longer linked to the contemplation of time's flow, but instead becomes the reflexive power of memory, the power to return and to recollect. The rediscovered time of primal insouciance where our hope is born, the "water of life." It is through this quest that time is inscribed in Egoyan's cinema, under the traits of childhood and remembrance.

*The Memory of Fire*: This consciousness of a time that emerges anew overwhelms us with its dazzling brilliance, in the manner of fire understood as a celestial force: the thunderbolt, the sign of Zeus's anger, shaking, burning, destroying, yet simultaneously engendering light, illuminating, rendering visible. Like the fires in *The Adjuster* that destroy homes, shatter the continuum of time, and amaze the victims, plunging them into a "state of shock" by uncovering what they had never before dared to say: "something had to change." The igneous element as dazzling brilliance also character-izes the arrow that Noah shoots in a kind of cathartic ritual — an attempt to end to this time of "quotidian simulacra" — against the billboard of the model home, which figures a kind of mythic Python, a facsimile that redoubles the factitiousness of the home he lives in. Brilliance as that which suspends time, postpones or dissolves it: a stopping power that allows nothing to endure, but lets new possibilities be envisaged in counter-point. Even Noah, the man of reconstruction in his ship-motel, begins to forget the threats of Zeus, discovering through his flame-touched victims the hope abandoned in Pandora's jar. Time becomes promise again. "All that is meant to protect us is bound to fall apart, bound to become contrived, useless and absurd. " (*Calendar*).

It is also by the inscription of our acts that Egoyan's images show us what we have forgotten about ourselves, by attaching to the emanations of an "imaging" body (as with Lance of *Speaking Parts*, an extra seeking a full-fledged role). The act becomes the sign of a still unspeakable body, in the quest to rediscover a memory of the senses, the memory of a body desiring like fire, here a human power which produces warmth (as underscored by the final image of *The Adjuster*, where Noah's reaches out toward the flames of the burning home). To this warmth is attached an erotic symbolism founded on an early scientific hypothesis for the production of fire through rubbing, that is, through love:[7] fire as a sexual symbol (idem, all back-and-forth movement, like that of 53 ▶ the seesaw between brother and sister in *Next of Kin*, or of the daughter in *The Adjuster*). Thus fire has a cathartic function, dilating and liberating bodies, breaking their chains, like the "intruder" in Pasolini's *Theorem* (echoed in *The Adjuster*[8]), who shakes apart the factitious universe of a bourgeois family by revealing them to each other through the carnal love that he dispenses, before disappearing.

This unbound time then opens to other possibilities, to other divides and exchanges. It is a time one chooses to live in: centered on the hearth, a "focal point" of domestic life[9] — fire in its proximity to light — which here stands as the intimacy of speech transmitted "from mouth to ear," engendering the filiation. It is through this quest for a focal point where speech could be rediscovered that the story of the "sons" unfolds. This filiation redoubles genetic descent: a "mythic" father is adjoined to the real one, a false father for a true hero's birth. Such is the case of Peter, the son in *Next of Kin*, who seeks to have himself adopted by an Armenian family, repeating his own birth in order to provoke a family rebirth through the return of the lost child. Or the case of Van, the son in *Family Viewing*, who seeks contact with his grandmother Armen (forgotten by the family in a hospital), so as to bring about the "rebirth" of his mother and attain a kind of hero's recognition. Van's traits may well conceal another metamorphosis of Dionysos: echoing the myth, he takes refuge beside his grandmother (Armen as the double of Rhea?), only to see his mother reappear at the end of the film, as in the legend where, at the close of his life on earth, Dionysos brought his mother forth from Hell (or in the film, from submission to the sadomasochist camera of the father), where she had sojourned after having been accidentally struck by the thunderbolts of her lover Zeus, as a consequence of one of Hera's ruses. As the myth tells us, it was Rhea who initiated Dionysos to the Mysteries, explaining how to break the chains of individuation, how to become "air, water, earth, and fire."[10]

The theme of filiation (which shows us the son's attempts to break the order of time as succession and chronological enchainment by infiltrating it with a "chronoscopic" time, "gathering the echoes of a living oblivion of memory") thus stands for an initiation 54 ▶

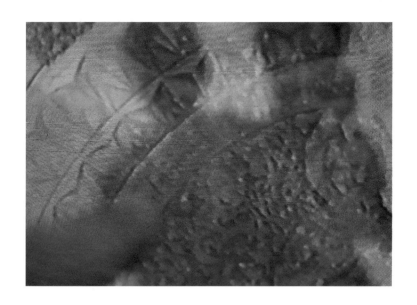

◄ 55 whose goal is the transmutation of a destiny. This mnemic impact which allows one to be elsewhere — both here and there — pulverizes the univocal nature of time, like the transmutation of fire as an element into an energy that volatilizes itself, giving access to the very matter of fire: ether, "the lion's fire, the energetics of the universal soul, wherein both the minerals and the bones of the ancestors are found."[11] Prometheus had stolen the seeds of fire's warmth (flame), the images have stolen its agency (light). "The soul of the dead" has fallen into the image where our memories will henceforth be materialized, because it is there that we perceive our organicity. It is this invisible partner that Clara convokes in *Speaking Parts* when she uses the projection of the video film to bring back her brother, dead for having given her his organs, but still living in the image, while she lives on from the gift of this dead body. The image as remembrance and mediator between the living and the dead becomes the matrix of the initial touch of time,[12] of the weight of history, of memory as the power of return: for "time is also ringed."[13] Whence the necessity for art to carry out the transformation (Phoenix reborn from the ashes) that can permit new alliances.

Egoyan's world plays on the ambivalence of the limit, not as what separates, cuts off or cuts short, but as a porous and tactile surface, thermic and coenaesthetic, the skin of the world: attractive, repulsive, intensive, the place of exchange.

*Of Words and Images*: The importance that Atom Egoyan accords to our modern tools of communication underscores their role in today's environment, where they occupy the place of our ancient gods. This "state of things" is imprinted with the "primitive" character of technology, permitting the exteriorization of imaginary figures nourished on the "hope" of Pandora's jar, and now released into a vast network of distribution. The "fantasmatic images" that interest Egoyan are related more to *expression* than *re*pression: the impersonal mode having taken over for strict silence, they are deployed through the anonymous networks of communication set up by our contemporary societies — "phone sex," address-exchange systems, private videos — which impress their form on a collective imagination tending more and more toward personalization, ◄ 56 even as society becomes more anonymous and reality more depersonalized.

What is more, our daily use of remote-control video for "channel-hopping" has introduced a new way of seeing, which telescopes our private images together with divinities and stars, fictions and history. What ensues is a fragmentation of time and a loss of the meaning of images, which disincarnate and autonomize into new mythic entities; but there is also a new reversibility of time, whereby one can return, stop, erase, and re-record.

Can one still truly speak of an image today, when it can be broadcast and retransmitted by television and satellite relays to the point where the stage is everywhere? When the frame, the limit that constitutes an image separated from the exterior/interior world, has become undecideable? Transmission is diffracted, a labyrinthic network is woven; where do our images come from?

This new imaginary register, conveyed over our communication networks by a mechanism of frustration/imitation, finally reduces the role of the imagination to a simple compensation, and thus contributes, through a counter-effect, to a progressive repression of metaphors. In this context, where the imagination finds itself coupled to discourse, one is again led to question images by attaching one's attention to the genesis of the processes of imagination within a unified experience of language. Now, metaphors considered as a "semantism of the imaginary"[14] show that a symbolic system constituting itself on the basis of myths — where the notion of symbolism can be extended beyond empirical conditions — partakes of a universal dimension. The symbolics of fire, at the origin of the primordial act of Promethean man freeing himself from the gods, allows for this redeployment of the imaginary, which can be divided and traversed anew.

This trajectory between the visibility of the world we live in and the vision of the world alive within us marks out the territory that Atom Egoyan explores, in a mirroring play of aberrant images that compose his cinema as a kind of theater of the absurd. Through these dual relationships that imitate the antagonsim of myth and logos, perpetuating the repetition of the same and its resultant disorders, we are again led to wonder about the mytho-logical "mis-understanding." Redoubling our everyday

57 ▶

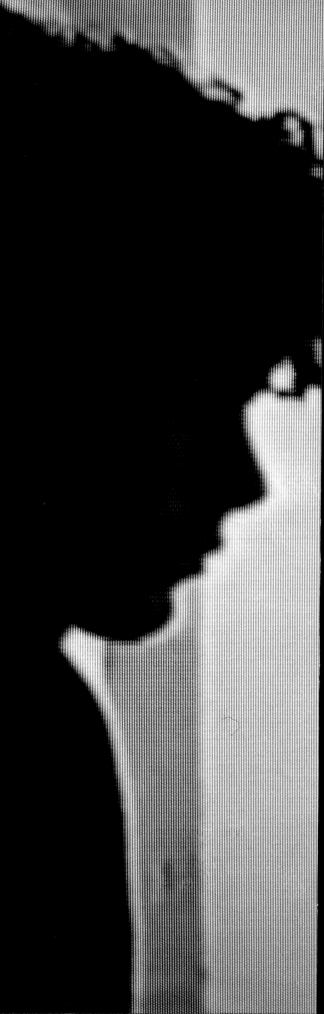

behaviors, Egoyan's references to mythology prove to be a metaphorical mode of decoding the ritual of our acts — or their "absurdism," whereby certain causes always go on producing the same effects. However, for him there do not seem to be two antagonistic ways of reading the world, but rather ambivalence and complementarity, as in the archaic time when myth and logos not only designated the sacred narrative concerning the gods and heroes, but also drew on the profane story of secret traditions transmitted "from mouth to ear": the oral traditions of lineages entrusted with a technique (like the blacksmiths) wherein our material imaginary has its origin. No longer believe in images: but know where they come from.

If in an initial moment the reference to myths constitutes a cosmic "expansion" of images, it also names the *topos* where the outlet of cosmic fire pours away into water, becoming speech that one gathers, and that gathers humans together: could anyone forget the fate of Narcissus, doomed to lose himself in an image that he burns to rejoin, all for having ignored the faroff appeals of Echo?

*The Place of the Spectator*: Through the inclusion of a spectator present in the image but able to break free and become an actor in his own right, Atom Egoyan's filmic space constitutes an interactive system that calls on the effective presence of ourselves, with-drawn in our silent voyeurism on the other side of the screen. For in fact, the image that interests Egoyan is the one projected by our gaze, redoubling the images of the world: he questions how we see these images and how we refilm them, like the father in *Family Viewing* partially erasing the family films to record his own fantasies. Atom Egoyan focuses on this ambivalence of the image in which the spectator, redoubled on the screen, watches himself projecting his mental images onto the images of the world. The cineast leads the viewer to replay this experience "live"; but here, the fantasmatic body is already the other who gazes upon it. And it is perhaps through this diffracted redoubling that the image extracted from ourselves materializes, becomes incarnate, and now begins to regard us — no longer as a fantasy, but as a witness to the movements whereby we drift away from the censorship of bodies and images. This redoubling pulverizes the notion of space and time in a kind of "vertigo" approaching the "dream state" that Egoyan claims for his films. His is a cinema where one no longer identifies only with the hero, but also with aspects of the image, with the cinegraphic body of the camera, with light itself — and with a desire for something, a desire to be something else: to accomplish this vague fusion of the self whereby the visible becomes solid, concrete. The body is in place before the screen, and it is clear that the organization has already been arranged. The demand for participation would seem to be no longer so much a demand for identification as for a sharing of affects.[15]

*To Have a Body*: Egoyan's cinema is also attached to underscoring a filmic process which alternates between the interlocking and the autonomization of the images. In the former case it is a matter of designating their frame in its association with diverse modes of capture (cinema, video, or photographic cameras); while in the latter, of revealing the nature of the medium, whose filmic or cathodic specificity has long since attached to modes of perception in the viewer, linked either to projection on the big screen (cinema) or to reception on the little one (television). Through this succession of viewpoints Atom Egoyan accentuates the ambivalence in the transmission of images. Knowing full well that his films will not only be shown in movie theaters, but will also be distributed in video cassettes for the television screen, he reverses the phenomenon by recording video images on film, to project television into the movie theater. And yet with this inversion it is less the frame than the medium, the physical support, which qualifies the image.

This sensitivity to the medium reminds us that film is also an affair of physical surface, of skin.* Egoyan studies this skin in the attempt to establish a genetic representation of each image, identifying the elements of the code that generates it in order to draw out it sense and its senses. Images that flake away to reveal the grain of the film or the video, through the movement and the nature of the camera's gaze: images no longer only seen but perceived as a tactile surface, as a textual matter wherein our acts are inscribed, both as concretions of thought and as materializations of language.

* As also indicated by the etymology of the French word for film, *pellicule*, from the Latin *pella*, skin. — Translator.

Thus Egoyan claims an emotional approach for his cinema, making the camera felt not through what it sees but through its way of looking, its way of choreographing space, of slipping from the skin of the film to the surface of bodies. This approach invests the image with affective intensities that bring the spectator into a tissue of relations, where he can give the image body again. For Egoyan, "seeing is also desiring to touch."[16] Here, the camera is co-present with the spectator's body, which it surprises in the domestic environment; but it is also a "tactile camera," reaching in, appropriating private images. The "intruder" here is the camera's gaze: its effects are destructive, insofar as it inhabits our environment, surveys us, steps into our place; but they are also salutary, since it objectifies or zooms in on our imaginary figures, revealing how we see the world, how we construct our mental images. The camera shows us what we don't see, what we don't know about ourselves. In this close-up vision introduced by the specular system of Atom Egoyan's cinema, the camera has become subjective and participates in the transmission of emotion. The images are resubstantialized through the experience of time and memory as antidotes to the images of an objectified body that does no more than advertise itself, disincarnated by modes of representation modeled on other images, themselves coded and reified by communication machines that defer contact. This memory of touch and of the body is evoked by Mimi in *The Adjuster* when she wonders why people sing in the shower: "It's one of the only times when we touch ourselves. *All* of ourselves. Do you think that's the reason?" Whence the need to remake a fluctuating skin to reach the body of the viewer, anaesthetized beneath the layers of images and the codes fused into them. An over-skin or excrescence that can be burnt away, like Seta's photos and Hera's warts in *The Adjuster*, or washed off by water, as Bubba explains to Mimi: "I thought of the reason why people sing in showers. It's got something to do with cleaning. The joy of washing things away.... Dirt. Hair. Dead skin. It makes me happy just to think about it." The

gesture/movement of the camera lingers on this film/skin, in order to cut through, to reestablish contact and exchange, thus giving rise to a theater of materials, no longer the site of an evocation of images in a representational space but a condensation of image and imagination in a co-belonging. This process generates an "intervallic" space, perceptive and intensive, where "the goal is to make the return of memory into the condition of a living forgetfulness, a double inscription which would not attempt to coincide with itself, but would hollow out surface regions where the body might glimpse unsuspected chances for survival."[17] Here, the tactile effects "do no refer to the eye but to the gaze, that is, to a desiring body, a sensitive and sensual body."[18] Between film and skin, image and spectator, the visible is actualized in its material contingency, carrying out this physical action of an image that comes closer, that touches us.

*Where to Live Physically?*[19] How can we inhabit the image and actualize our memory within it as invisible time, reestablishing the communication between image and imagination, between the soul and the body, in the face of this simulacrum which reproduces the same model indefinitely: the fantasmatic screen? What is called for here is a space to live in, and no longer to reconstruct, unlike the model home of *The Adjuster* where the surrounding emptiness left one supposing possible extensions, at least until the promoters went bankrupt. Egoyan's cinema explores man and his tools of communication through the metaphorical dimension of the machine, attempting to redesign a body between meaning and sensibility, a body that can reconcile the technical and the biological in a new relationship to the world.

A skin that moults and reestablishes contact. Change the skin to change the body: unchain oneself from the mystifying power of images, which consists in putting oneself in another's skin, or produces an oblivion of the body that then becomes fantasmatic or simply gives itself up, turns into a common coin of exchange, like the body of Lance insuring his continued presence at the hotel while offering an advantage to his passing female clients; or like the reified body on display as a spectacle, the body of Clara's brother, the donor of organs (*Speaking Parts*).

59 ▶

This skin, which we must reach to regenerate a body, evokes the mediator between gods and men, the linking principle between light and shadow: Hermes, who brought Pandora to earth on the orders of Zeus. The skin and Hermes (a global communications agency[20]): both at the crossroads of relations.

This passage through Hermes brings us to the forge of Hephaestos, the legitimate son of Hera and Zeus who cast Prometheus in chains. On his father's orders this master of metals and fire, of artisans and the arts, modeled Pandora's body and Zeus's thunderbolt, and with Cyclops' help created many other masterpieces. The forge of Hephaestos — in relation with the subterranean fires, in communion with the heavens — could be a metaphor of the *hearth*, regrouping the dramatic chorus at the center of Atom Egoyan's cinema; and indeed, Egoyan situates many scenes of his films underground, like the hotel laundry room where the heroine works in *Speaking Parts*, the studio where Lance joins her at the end of the film, the projection room of the image censors in *The Adjuster*, and so forth. Was it not Hephaestos who took vengeance on his mother Hera by enchaining her to a throne, until Dionysos freed her and gave her drink? Art as inoxication: to surprise Hephaestos.

Through the symbolics of fire and the return to a forge deserted by the gods, Atom Egoyan invites us to come nearer to the hearth, to dilate and regenerate our bodies at the focal point: like the chorus of Greek tragedy or of the medieval mystery plays, where the spectator was invited to step into the playing space or *magic circle*, to become actor as well. This focal point is also the lens of the camera that Egoyan leads us to traverse, by placing a double of ourselves at the heart of the drama, a double who becomes an actor and tries to shake off his chains, the better to attach and intertwine, to transmit "from mouth to ear" again — for to love, to desire, is to communicate.

60 ▶

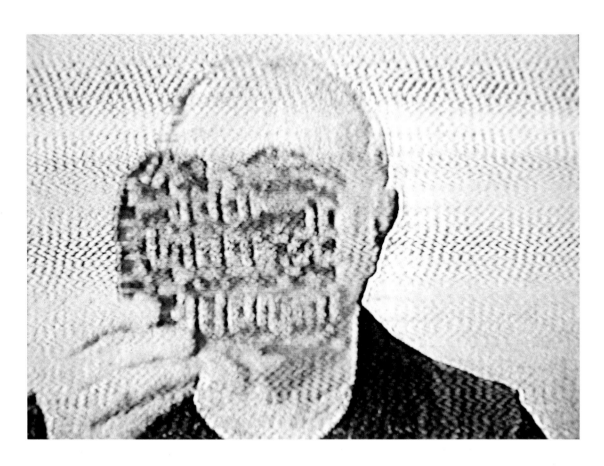

# VIDEO LETTERS

The interview between Atom Egoyan and Paul Virilio took place at a distance, by video cassette.

The first cassette containing Paul Virilio's questions was recorded in Paris, June 18, 1993.
Atom Egoyan answered from Toronto, July 22,1993.

*Atom, I'm going to pose my questions in the void of the video and you can answer the same way. It's strange, but it closely resembles your work.*

FIRST QUESTION: *According to my friend Serge Daney, who died of AIDS just one year ago, "cinema and video could only be mutually exclusive." I have the feeling that your opinion is different. I even have the impression that your works are veritable "video installations" (or "hyper installations"), no longer set up in museum or commercial galleries, but inside the film itself. Is that true? Are you the first "videast" to no longer find free space, or the first "cine-videast" to choose filmic space?*

I was very intrigued by your notion that video as presented in the films I've made functions very much like an installation work. I think that invites the whole question of reflexive or self-reflexive response to a space, how gallery space operates on the viewer, the ritual of going into a space, of seeing art presented within a space, and how very often in a film we are not conscious of the path that we have to go through in order to receive images. They imprint themselves on our consciousness in a very immediate and effortless way. They invite our immediate participation, and we are not aware of the process of having to traverse the space in order to enter into the state that the artist is wishing to express.

What I choose to do by presenting video images within the film is to make the viewer very aware that the image is a construct. The image is a mechanical process of projection, and the viewers are made aware of that process by seeing the video image within the film image. This invites a very curious question, which is: does the converse process work, when a film image is shown on a video screen? The answer is no, of course; most of the TV movies that we see are shot on film, but are projected to us through video and become documents which find their life on a video screen. But when I make a video image and project it on film, the viewer is very aware of how frail and delicate and precarious that image is. And this a very interesting space to work with. I think that the two mediums are obviously married to each other in their

◄ 61

◄ 62

physical properties and in their ability to represent reality, but the video image has associations which are far more quotidian, far more domestic and less mystified. There is still a mystification which exists around the filmmaking process. When people see a projected image, they're seeing something larger than life, something which is beyond them and therefore invites a very specific type of identification. When people see a video image, the first response is that it is something that *they themselves* could make. It is not full of the same mystification and therefore it is far easier, I think, to be suspicious of a video image, to wonder what its value is, especially in a dramatic context. We're all aware of the values of video as an archival instrument, very much like it is being used right now to trace the images of our conversation in an archival and practical way. But in terms of how it is able to function as a means of creative expression, it opens up many many avenues.

So I'm not really capable of discussing whether I'm a videast who is transcending the barriers of my form or a cineast who is exploring new territories. I think there are many artists who have done it before me, Godard being the most obvious example. So I don't see myself necessarily as being an innovator or as the first person to ask these questions. But perhaps because the films are dealing with the process of memory and of the construct of memory, with how we are able to manipulate our own state of consciousness in order to serve or to enhance our relationships to one another and to distort our relationships to one another, perhaps all these issues become more pointed, more specific in the work I'm doing. I hope that answers the first question.

SECOND QUESTION: *Maurice Blanchot spoke not too long ago of a literary space that is irreducible to literature. Can it be said that what now interests Atom Egoyan is a filmic space irreducible to cinema? Today, with end of the notion of "intervals" — intervals of space and time, which organize space — and the rise of the instantaneous "interfaces" of the video signal, can one still speak of filmic representation?*

To respond to your second question, I think it is very important to state first of all that the principle by which I construct my films is based very much on the notion of characters in the late twentieth century being completely overwhelmed by their place in a society which is constructed on image. The whole delineation of personality and the conduct of personality through the society become very precarious. It becomes difficult to distinguish between natural patterns of behavior which represent our true intentions and patterns of behavior which we create to represent our intentions as we believe will best serve our image.

This is a very complex discourse, but what it suggests in relationship to your question perhaps is that our own ability to deconstruct our personalities, or, I should say, *my intention* to deconstruct ideas of personality *on screen* is informed by a very emotional response to the predicament my characters find themselves in. The best way for me to represent that split, that breakdown of personality, is by showing in a very mechanical and literal way these characters in the process of creating images of each other, or of having a fantasy life based on a mechanical principle — that being their own ability to make images of each other or to substitute images of each other or to alter images of each other. In this sense, my characters create a pattern of discourse which suggests a level of awareness and a level of self-conscious response to their alienation or to their fractured state.

I think that the references that you're making in terms of the space of cinema are in my view perhaps confined to a very fixed notion of a delineation between the properties of the film image and the video image. I don't see this distinction. I see the video image as being something which, as I said before, is very accessible and is very comprehensible at a certain level. And yet its effect on our psyche and its effects on our way of thinking about ourselves and society around us are very profound, very elusive and complex. Therefore, to take one medium which is very straightforward, very literal, and to place that in a format of another medium which is mystified and very much outside of our experience — that being the film image — is an idea that can be extremely rich in its metaphor and its ability to work both against itself and within itself at the same time. Film and video are obviously both imagistic mediums, but they have completely different suggestions. And of course, one is more contemplative than the other. I suggest that the video image is more contemplative because we have to make a very conscious effort to transcend the everyday or — as I said before — "quotidian" nature of that image. For that image to transport us to another realm it has to be contextualized in a more specific way than the film image. The film image by its very nature transcends a quotidian response. It is much easier to create a myth around a human face when it is projected on a film screen than when it is presented on a video screen. But to take that video image of a face and place it on to the film screen creates a very elusive rapport, because you have to identify the properties of both mediums and understand why the video is being presented within the territory of the film image. What is its purpose there, what is its value? And that invites a whole questioning of the nature of that face as a construct, which is very exciting in a dramatic and psychological analysis of character.

THIRD QUESTION: *In a recent interview, you stated that pornography plays a major role in the vision of the new sexuality. Can you explain to me what kind of "pornography" is happening when video gazes on video? Does the appearance of "vision without a gaze" abolish obscenity?*

What is particularly suggestive about a pornographic vision as it pertains to the video image is that it immediately suggests an allusion to the person who made that image. We are just as aware of the person behind the camera as we are of the image we see in front of us. This accounts for something which may or may not be popular in France right now, but which in North America is the current fad: amateur pornography, which is pornography made by people in their own homes, then sold and distributed in shops. People are very attracted by this type of pornography because it is thrilling to imagine the person and the events that led to this specific act of videotaping one's lover or one's friends in a sexual act. It suggests a little something we're capable of. To go back to what I was speaking of before, it is a strip-

ping away of the mystification of the image. The image is not something which becomes an object of idolatry, but rather it is a very functional statement and an expression of a very simple emotional need. Then the question becomes: what is the context in which such an image is viewed? And by placing this very simple and emotive gesture — the video image — in the context of a film image, do you then transport it into a realm where the act of watching reflects back on itself and therefore suggests a totally different response? What I find exciting about this question is to wonder what would happen if I were to transcribe one of these amateur home videos onto film and project it in a film theater. Would that reduce its excitement, would it all of a sudden become something other than what it was intended for, which was to be a record of a very domestic ritual? I believe it would.

In the films I've made, there are moments where we're witnessing a sexual response through the video image. I think I'm accentuating the obscenity because I'm taking what is intended as a very intimate and direct gesture and I am all of a sudden making it into some-thing more, and by doing so, I am robbing it of a certain dignity. I'm making the viewers aware of the fact that they are watching some-thing unfold which was *not* meant directly for their eyes, and at the same time I'm reducing the capability of voyeuristic response, because I am suggesting that *I* as the filmmaker have already robbed the watching of this image of its voyeuristic intent. By reprojecting it, I'm not allowing the viewer to feel that this is something they have discovered. I have already discovered it for them, so what then is the value of a sex image? I believe that perhaps answers the question.

I'd like to go on with this third question though, because I think it touches on something which I find very exciting, which is the whole notion of who has privileged access to this source of the intention behind the creation of an image. Right now I'm making a video document to send to you, so that *you* can watch it in the privacy of your home and try to decipher my response to your questions. It is intended for your eyes. If you are then to make a video document of this image, if you are to reposition another lens onto this image that I am transmitting to you, you are appropriating not only my imagined gaze, my imagined regard to you, but you are also creating an entirely new context for the question of why this image was made in the first place. You are able, by the simple act of rephotographing it, or retraining a lens against it, to transmogrify the intention of what the image was made for.

How does this relate to the pornographic image? One of the strongest impulses in the pornographic image is the idea that you are seeing something which you should not be seeing; that you have access to an image which is somehow not intended for your eyes. But to then rephotograph or retranslate that back into another image is to reduce the pornographic object of its power, to alter its intentionality, and by doing so, to open up an entirely different level of discourse.

FOURTH QUESTION: *Observing your films, one inevitably recalls the phrase of Paul Klee: "Now objects are aware of me." Now I no longer see the world, but things contemplate me. Can it be said that a new kind of robotics is emerging today, an "automation of perception" (and not solely of production),* *which is foreshadowed in your work? Are you the one who brings about the disappearance of the cameraman in favor of the machine, or are you the first cineast of the new filmic representation?*

I think that we have viewed so many human beings framed against so many walls, so many rooms, and so many life styles, in so many patterns, in so many relationships — to the objects which define those life styles, which define those very particular contexts — that we are now in a state where we identify ourselves with the objects that we choose to surround ourselves with. We have to, at a certain point, and perhaps subconsciously we imagine ourselves being photographed, being represented, and being placed in a context where those objects define our personality.

And in that sense, yes, it is very true that these objects look back *at us*. Because we are looking back at them. Calvino actually brought that out in a short story about a photographer, where he suggests that life really becomes meaningless unless it is photographed, unless it is capable of being photographed. And I think that perhaps one of the issues I'm trying to deal with in *Calendar* is this whole notion of something being substantiated as it works in a photographic way.

But it is not the notion of being able to keep the photograph as a souvenir, as an object of reflection, which is perhaps the older view of what a photographic identification meant. Rather, it is the very fact that a context is provided for and is defined by the parameters of what a lens sees; and that to place yourself within those parameters enhances your own identification.

I think that in terms of how this works with the patterns of memory and the patterns of our sense of shared experience, things become extremely complex because we have to be able to see our lives as artifacts which can be exchanged, whereby I can make this artifact of myself, this icon of myself which I would exchange with you, knowing full well that my actions, my words, have an importance beyond what they mean, because of the fact that they are being documented. But the extension of that is for me to somehow imagine every moment of my life, every word that is coming out of my mouth as being suitable for the process of documentation, because the process of documentation defines our modern sense of what it means to lead a truly rich experience.

FIFTH AND LAST QUESTION: *After the reign of living actors, where men, women, and animals took all the roles, it seems to me that with you (and Cronenberg) we're witnessing a transfer of roles to inert objects or to machines, to motorized devices: washing machines, aquariums, TV monitors, and so forth. Can it be said that in your films there are no more "passive" instruments and that all machines are not only "active" but are actors too, and sometimes even "stars"!!??*

*Here I'm thinking of the roles that you often give to your camera. It is no longer, I believe, a matter of a simple "recording box" for the film; the camera is the leading actor, whose emancipation and indeed autonomy you are seeking.*

PERSONAL COMMENTS ON YOUR WORK:

*What I prefer in your filmic writing is its geometry (I'm weighing my words), the "play of mirrors" between the image and the thing, and above all the new type of perspective: a* perspective which is no longer the real space of the Quattrocento, but a perspective developed from the real time of the shot and of its retransmission. For example, there is the moment in Calendar when the actress extends a glass of wine to the cameraman filming her, or the "handing over of the passport" between the local Armenian and the Armenian behind the lens — yourself, I believe, in this case!

In your work, there is no longer forward and within, as in most classical films; there is above all forward and behind. You film "in reverse gear," with the risks of invisibility that implies, with the fall into oblivion. Maybe you're lacking an object: the rear-view mirror or the back-up lamps... With you, the film is no longer "in the film"; it is around, in the surroundings, in the mental image of the viewer... Sometimes I would like to no longer see your films head-on, in a frontal way, but in profile, to better grasp the cuts, which are not geologic but geometric.

Contrary to mural painting, cinema has never been tempted by anamorphosis. Despite Abel Gance, the disintegration of the screen has never taken place; but you can do it. Go ahead, do it, but above all don't ever let "virtual space" (cyberspace) destroy you: the best pair of spectacles, the best imaging helmet, is memory. And as Norman O. Spear explains, "The content of memory is a function of the speed of forgetting."

I would now like to show you an object: a dead memory which itself forgets nothing. This memory is a microprocessor, an integrated circuit, which was cut out in the form of Tables of the Law by a friend of mine during the Gulf war. I offer it to you through the intermediary of the image. But let me remind you, it is a dead memory.

For me there is nothing simple about the process of making images. While I am very seduced by the act of making an image, I am also very very aware of all the contradictions involved in making images of other human beings, representing those images and defining those images by the mechanical properties of the lens. If we accept the view that in this time, at this point in our society, we all understand the value of a lens, then filmmakers cannot use that same piece of glass and pretend there is something innocent and naive about the process they are engaged in.

For me, the act of filming something goes hand in hand with the idea that *somebody* is filming that image. There is no point in being coy or being simplistic about this and saying that you are just representing people. You are also providing another character which is the person behind that lens. In all my films there are very important characters, or even a central character who is missing, who is not in the drama. I choose the camera very often as being the spirit or the embodiment of that missing person. And it's a very suggestive and profound experience to realize that we are seeing a number of human beings gobble up their lives, all of them in contemplation of a character or an identity which they are looking for, and that the lens with which you are regarding these people might hold the secrets of the very thing that they feel is lacking in their own lives. This puts the viewers in a very exciting position whereby they then have to identify what it is in their own process of looking at these people, of watching these people behave on screen, that might provide some response for these fictitious characters. And of course that whole discourse can only go on within the imagination of the viewer. There is nothing which is literally there. What I am inviting is an acknowledgment of the fact that we can view human beings as they are represented, and as they become objects by that process of representation, and still preserve a level of rapport with these screen images as they relate to our own expectation, our own wish for fulfillment.

In classical Hollywood terms, this wish for fulfillment would be somehow provided to us by means of screen identification, that is to say we would look at a screen image, we would identify ourselves into that screen image and lose ourselves for the period of time that we are watching a film. And this is actually the classical way of looking at cinema: cinema as the opportunity to transcend our lives by somehow projecting ourselves onto a screen for the period of time that an image is being projected.

I think that it is now possible to find that same level of excitement and transcendence through an identification of the screen image as something which is *objectified*. Because that is closer to our experience now and it answers more vitally a question which I think is invited by the screen image: why do we need to look? Why do we need to watch anything? In a world where we are overwhelmed by images, what is the purpose of seeing something else? Are we looking to expand our vocabulary? Are we looking for entertainment? And can we be entertained by something which we are too plugged into, which we are so completely accustomed to? Where is the entertainment value? What is the purpose of seeing something else? And if we are able to address that question and to examine our own need to see more, to in fact redefine our own curiosity by a new type of exploration of the screen image, then I think this opens up very exciting avenues for the dramatist. What it actually does is to create an entirely new persona for us to work with. Maybe the lens becomes a redefinition of the classical Greek chorus. Maybe the lens is the new chorus for our drama, it is the thing which comments on the actions of the principal actors, but contextualizes them and invites our own sense of what it is we expect from these people, from these mere mortals. It is the closest we come to finding the voice of the Gods, which is again the notion of the chorus. It becomes our oracle.

It is much like the experience of talking to you by this very strange process: I suppose I feel as though I'm addressing this lens in front of me as an oracle. Because I know that it will provide you with a projection which you will have to respond to. It's very frustrating in some ways to be speaking this way because I am in such admiration of your work; I'm honored by the time you've taken to ask me these questions. Thank you so much.

Now, after your amazing gift, I would like to give you a gift by video as well, one that also deals with time and with the very potent possibilities of an image. This is the pregnant belly of my wife which is holding a seven-and-a-half month child. And by the time we will be there in November, perhaps I will be able to present a child in front of the lens, as opposed not only to a child behind the lens, but also to the child behind the lens of this belly and this flesh.

I'm sure that the levels of irony and intimacy which I am expressing to you right now will leave a very nice sense of closure to our discourse. Goodbye.

65 ▶

# FILMOGRAPHY

## HOWARD IN PARTICULAR

1979

*Screenplay, images and Editor* : Atom Egoyan. *Music* : Garth Lambert. *Interprétation* : Carman Guild, Anthony Saunders, Arthur Bennet. *Production* : Ego Film Arts
14 mn/16 mm/ N&B

*A large company tries to steamline the retirement process by compressing the entire operation into six minutes... without inviting guests to the party. Using an effective juxtaposition of objective and subjective camera angles, Howard in particular examines the strange and obsessive nightmares of one such retiree and his submission to dismissal.*

## AFTER GRAD WITH DAD

1980

*Screenplay, images and Editor* : Atom Egoyan. *Music* : Garth Lambert. *Interprétation* : Alan Toff; Anthony saunders; Lynda-Mary Greene. *Production* : Ego Film Arts
25 mn/16 mm/ Colour

*After Grad with Dad examines the paranoid perceptions of a nervous young man who, upon accidently arriving at his girl friend's home half an hour earlier than expected, is forced to maintain a conversation with the girl friend's father*

## PEEP SHOW

1981

*Screenplay, images and Editor* : Atom Egoyan. *Music and sound effects*: Matthew Poulakakis, David Rokeby. *Interprétation* : John Ball, Clarke Letemendia, David Littlejohn. *Production* : Ego Film Arts
7 mn/16 mm/ B&W and colour

*Peep Show demonstrates a form of pornography that intrudes upon a customer's more intimate desires. Using an usual and innovative colour technique, the film manipulates the ordinary into the unexpected, culminating in a peep show in which the viewer becomes the subject of exploitation.*

## OPEN HOUSE

1982

*Screenplay and Editor* : Atom Egoyan. *Camera* : Peter Mettler. *Music* : David Rokeby.
*Interprétation*: Ross Fraser (Frank), Michael Marshall (Michael), Sharon Cavanaugh (Maureen), Hovsep Yeghoyan (Mr. Odahrian), Alberta Davidson (Mrs. Odahrian), Bruce Bell (Man on the street).
*Production* : Ego Film Arts with the assistance of the Ontario Arts Council
25 mn/16 mm/Colour

*A disturbed real-estate agent tries to sell a dilapidated house to a young couple. It soon becomes apparent that the agent is the son of the people who built the house, and that the entire ritual of selling is a bizarre method of sustaining pride in a household drained of self-respect.*

## NEXT OF KIN

1984

*Screenplay and Editor* : Atom Egoyan. *Dir. Phot.* : Peter Mettler. *Sound* : Clark McCarron. *Artistic Director* : Ross Nichols
*Interprétation*: Patrick Tierney (Peter /Bedros), Berge Fazlian (George Deryan), Sirvart Fazlian (Sonya Deryan), Arsinée Khanjian (Azah Deryan), Margaret Loveyes (Mrs Foster), Thomas Tierney (Mr Foster).
*Production* : Ego Film Arts
72 mn/16 mm/Colour

*Catonically unhappy with his family life, a young man named Peter Foster undergoes video therapy with his parents. One day, while studying tapes at the hospital, he sees the tapes of an Armenian family who feel guilty about surrendering their own son, while still an infant, to a foster home. Peter decides to present himself to this family as their lost son, to finally act out a role different for the one assigned to him in his own life. Filled with haunting images of travel and displacement, Next of Kin, reveals a young WASP's response to a working-class Armenian culture and discourses on the range of roles that life allows us to play*

## MEN : A PASSION PLAYGROUND

1985

*Screenplay* : Gail Harris after his poem "Men". *Conception, Image and Editor* : Atom Egoyan. *Music* : Matthew Poulakakis, Perry Domzella
*Interprétation*: Gail Harris. *Production* : Ego Film Arts
7 mn/16 mm/Colour

*Perched at the top of a playground apparatus, poet Gail Harris, dressed as a priestess, intones an intensive cataloguing of all types of romantic males. Stretched in a semi-circle below her, men dressed in garb ranging business suits to tracks suits give homage to her while chanting "men, men". This poetic short is a riposte to the clichés of rock videos.*

## IN THIS CORNER

1985

*Screenplay* : Paul Gross. *Image* : Kenneth Gregg. *Editor* : Myrtle Virgo. *Music* : Eric Robertson
*Interprétation* : Robert Wisden, Patrick Tierney, Brenda Bazinet
*Production* : Alan Burke for CBC
60 mn/16 mm/Colour/Television

*A Toronto boxer, proud of his Irish heritage, is persuaded by the IRA to smuggle a terrorist back to Ireland with his fight crew. Questions of honour and loyalty are in the forefront of this moody thriller, which is punctuated by well-realized fight scenes of documentary-like intensity.*

## THE FINAL TWIST

1987

*Screenplay* : Jim Beaver, d'après une nouvelle de William Bankier
*Interprétation*: Martin Landau, Robert Wisden, Ann-Marie Mac Donald
*Production* : John Slan for "Alfred Hitchcock Presents"
30 mn/16 mm/Colour/Television

*Special effects artists stage an emergency in order to destroy their despicable boss. Working within a typically ironic Hichcockian tale, Egoyan goes beyond the genre to create a realistic depiction of the workings in a small film-production house. Landau and MacDonald are particularly effective as the womanizing petty film tyrant and the artisan who constructs his "final twist."*

## FAMILY VIEWING

1987

*Screenplay* : Atom Egoyan. *Dir. Phot.* : Robert McDonald. *Caméra* : Peter Mettler. *Editor* : Bruce McDonald and Atom Egoyan. *Sound* : Ross Redfern. *Music* : Michael Danna. *Artistic Dir.* : Linda Del Rosario. *Sets* : Ian Grieg. *Costume* : Matti Sevink
*Interprétation*: David Hemblen (Stan), Aidan Tierney (Van), Gabrielle Rose (Sandra), Arsinée Khanjian (Aline), Selma Keklikian (Armen), Jeanne Sabourin (Aline's mother), Rose Sarkisyan (Van's mother), Vasag Baghboudarian.
*Production* : Ego Film Arts with the participation of the Ontario Film Development Corporation, the Canada Council and the Ontario Arts Council.
86 mn/16mm/Colour

*This story of mistaken and found identities is set in a nursing home, a condominium and a telephone-sex establishment. Using a collection of video images - television, pornography, home movies and surveillance - the film observes the breakdown and restauration of a dislocated family. Darkly humorous and unpredictible, Family Viewing is a complex journey into a world of brutality and sentiment.*

## LOOKING FOR NOTHING

1988

*Screenplay* : Atom Egoyan. *Dir. phot.* : Andrew Binnington; *Editor* : Bruce Griffin.
*Interprétation*: Aaron Ross Fraser, Damir Andrei, Arsinée Khanjian, Hrant Alianak
*Production* : Paul da Silva and Anne O'Brien for "Inside Stories"/Toronto Talkies
30 mn/16 mm/Colour/Television

*Pandemonium strikes an Armenian gathering celebrating multiculturalism when the Provincial Security Force attempts to crack a conspiracy against the visiting premier. This look at contemporary Canadian cultural mores features a set-piece in which security operators are made to dress in ethnic garb in order to infiltrate an official diner.*

## SPEAKING PARTS

### 1989

*Screenplay* : Atom Egoyan. *Dir. Phot.* : Paul Sarossy. *Editor* : Bruce McDonald. *Music* : Mychael Danna. *Sound* : Steven Munro. *Artistic Director* : Linda Del Rosario. *Costumes* : Maureen Del Degan.
*Interprétation*: Michael McManus (Lance), Arsinée Khanjian (Lisa), Gabrielle Rose (Clara), David Hemblen (producer), Tony Nardi (Eddy), Patricia Collins (house keeper), Gerard Parkes (father), Jacqueline Samuda (Trish), Peter Krantz (Ronnie).
*Production* : Ego Film Arts with the participation of Telefilm Canada, the Ontario Film Development Corporation, Academy Pictures (Rome) and Film four International (London).
92 mn/35 mm/Colour
*"I have worked in a hotel for five years. I have worked in film for ten. Both of these professions involve the creation of illusion. In one, the territory of illusion is a room. In the other it is a screen. People move in and out of rooms. Actors move in and out of screens; Speaking Parts explores a terrain that moves between rooms and screens; a terrain of memory and desire. Somewhere in the passage from a room to a screen, a person is transformed into an image. I am fascinated by this crucial moment, and by the contradictions involved in making images of people.".* Atom Egoyan

## THE AJUSTER

### 1991

*Screenplay* : Atom Egoyan. *Dir. Phot.* : Paul Sarossy. *Editor* : Susan Shipton. *Music* : Mychael Danna.

*Sound* : Steven Munro. *Production designers* : Linda Del Rosario and Richard Paris. *Costumes* : Maya Mani
*Interprétation*: Elias Koteas (Noah), Arsinée Khanjian (Hera), Maury Chaykin (Bubba), Gabrielle Rose (Mimi), Jennifer Dale (Arianne), David Hemblen (Bert), Rose Sarkisyan (Seta), Armen Kokorian (Simon), John Gilbert (doctor).
*Production* : Ego Film Arts with the participation of Telefilm Canada, the Ontario Film Development Corporation and Alliance Communications.
102 mn/35 mm/Colours/Dolby Stéréo
*"I have made a film that concerns an insurance adjuster, some film censors, an ex-football player, an aspiring cheerleader, a podiatrist, an actress, a lamp merchant, a butterfly collector and the devoted staff of a large motel. Everyone is doing what they are doing for a reason, which is never the reason. I wanted to make a film about believable people doing believable things in an unbelievable way."* Atom Egoyan
*The Renders are in the ajustment business. Noah is an insurance adjuster who takes care of psychological - and physical- needs of his shocked clients. Hera, his wife, is a cultural adjuster : she works at the Provincial Censor Board. When a bizarre couple pays them to vacate their home for a "film shoot", the Renders takes up residence in the motel that houses Noah's clients and discover just how malajusted their lives -and those of others - can be.*

## MONTRÉAL VU PAR... six variations sur un thème
### (MONTREAL SEXTET)

### 1992

*Directors* : Patricia Rozema, Jacques Leduc, Michel Brault, Atom Egoyan, Léa Pool, Denys Arcand.
*Production* : Denise Robert, Doris Girard, Yves Rivard.
*Executive Producers* : Michel Houle, Peter Sussman.

*Episode 4* : "En passant"
*Screenplay* : Atom Egoyan. *Dir.phot.* : Eric Cayla. *Editor* : Susan Shipton. *Music* : Mychael Danna. *Sound* : Steven Munro.
*Interprétation*: Maury Chaykin, Arsinée Khanjian.
20mn/35mm/Colour
*A customs Officer steals one of the luggage tags of a pictogram designer arriving in Montreal, then sketches him and adds the drawing to her collection of "clients". The designer sets off from his hotel with an audio tour of Montreal on his walkman, almost running into the Customs Officer as he wanders through the city. Witty use of pictograms and a sensual response to the environment of a festive Montreal mark a gentle, philosophical interlude in Montreal vu par and in Egoyan's career.*

## GROSS MISCONDUCT

### 1992

*Screenplay* : Paul Gross from the book by Martin O'Malley. *Director of photography* : Brian Hebb. *Editor*: Gordon McClellen. *Music* : Mychael Danna.
*Interprétation*: Daniel Kash, Peter MacNeill, Linda Garanson, Doug Hughes, Lenore Zann
*Production* : Alan Burke pour CBC
120 mn/16 mm/Colour/Television

*The violent life of hockey player Brian "Spinner" Spencer was marked by drugs, infidelity and murder. Egoyan and scenarist Paul Gross turn this true story into a meditation on the codes of masculinity that delimited Spencer's career and life. Using titles such as "Trouble in Paradise", "What's Bred in the Bone", and "Sudden Death Overtime" as chapter headings, they transform a potentially tawdry tale into an essay on the Canadian gothic male.*

## CALENDAR

### 1993

*Screenplay and Editor* : Atom Egoyan. *Dir. phot.*: Norayr Kasper.

*Music* : Hohn Grimaldi. *Sound* : Steven Munro.
*Interprétation*: Arsinée Khanjian (translator); Ashot Adamian (driver); Atom Egoyan (photographer); Michelle Bellerose; Nathalia Jasen; Susan Hamann; Steva Kohli; Viva Tsvetnova; Rula Said; Annie Szamosi; Anna Pappas; Amanda Martinez; Diane Kofri (the guests).
*Co-producer* : Arsinée Khanjian.
*Production* : Ego Fim Arts; Produced with the participation of ZDF German Télévision and The Arménian National Cinématheque
75 mn/16 mm/Colour

*A Toronto photographer invites a different woman to have dinner with him each month. At the end of each meal, the guest makes a phone call to her lover and speaks passionately in a foreign language. The photographer's reveries reveal that his wife has left him for the man who guided their tour through Armenia, where they collected images for a calendar. Widly humorous and sensual, Calendar is Egoyan's most emotionally direct film.*

## EXOTICA

### 1993

*Screenplay* : Atom Egoyan. *Editor* : Susan Shipton. *Dir. phot* : Paul Sarossy. *Production designers* : Linda Del Rosario and Richard Paris.
*Interprétation*: Bruce Greenwood; Mia Kirshner; Elias Koteas; Arsinée Khanjian; Don Mc Kellar; David Hemblen.
*Production* : Ego Fim Arts
*Interprétation*Exotica, *Egoyan continues to explore his fascination with human relationships, the perilous nature of sexual love, the seduction of voyeurism and the ideology of the "family". The film is an insightful exploration into how we construct our own realities and illusions, and devise our own identities in an attempt to create a comfortable space for ourselves in the world. The narrative of Exotica centres around a night club, an opera house, and an exotic pet store.*

# BIBLIOGRAPHY

**66** ▶

**SPEAKING PARTS**

– 24 IMAGES, « Au-delà des images », Gérard Grugeau, mai 1989

– LE QUOTIDIEN DE PARIS, « L'exil perpétuel », 19 mai 1989

– LIBÉRATION, « Déréglement d'images », P.G., 20-21 mai 1989

– POSITIF, « La vidéo mode d'emploi », François Ramasse, n° 343, septembre 1989

– SÉQUENCES, « Rôles parlants », Martin Girard, n°144, janvier 1990

– *Speaking Parts*, Atom Egoyan (Toronto: Coach House Press, 1993)

**THE AJUSTER**

– LE CINÉPHAGE, « Qui est *in*? Qui est *out*? », Vincent Lebrun, n° 2

– LE CINÉPHAGE, « Vidéodrames », interview with Elisabeth Feret et Vincent Lebrun, n° 2, novembre 1991

– LE QUOTIDIEN DE PARIS, « L'arc de l'inconscient », Marc Joyeux, 27 novembre 1991

– LIBÉRATION, « Atom Egoyan : On n'est pas sûr de ce qu'on voit », interview with Philippe Vecchi, 28 novembre 1991

– LIBÉRATION, « *The Ajuster*, assurances sur le vide », Gérard Lefort, 28 novembre 1991

– SÉQUENCES, « *The Ajuster*, l'expert en sinistre », Elie Castiel, n°156, janvier 1992

– SIGHT & SOUND, « Burning Down The House, » Amy Taubin, juin 1992

– TÉLÉRAMA, « Mon Kafka au Canada », interview with Gérard Delorme, novembre 1991

**FAMILY VIEWING**

– LE MONDE, « Prises de vue en famille », Michel Braudeau, 8 juin 1989

– LES CAHIERS DU CINÉMA, F. Strauss, n°421, juin 1989

– LIBÉRATION, « Une vue de famille », 7 juin 1989

– POSITIF, « Brulantes solitudes », Olivier De Bruyn, n°370, décembre 1991

– POSITIF, « Jeux de miroirs », interview with Philippe Rouyer, n°370, décembre 1991

– POSITIF, « La vidéo mode d'emploi », François Ramasse, n° 343, septembre 1989

## *General Articles*

– 24 IMAGES, « Les élans du coeur », interview with Gérard Grugeau, décembre 1989

– 24 IMAGES, « Entretien avec Atom Egoyan », Julia Reschop, n° 67, 1993

– LES INROCKUTIBLES, « Théorie de l'Atom », interview with Samuel Blumenfeld, n°46, juin 1993

– SÉQUENCES, « Atom Egoyan », interview with Elie Castiel, n°144, janvier 1990

– FILM COMMENT, « Up and Atom », Amy Taubin, novembre/décembre 1989

**67** ▶ – CINE ACTION, « Scanning Egoyan », Cameron Bailey, printemps 1989

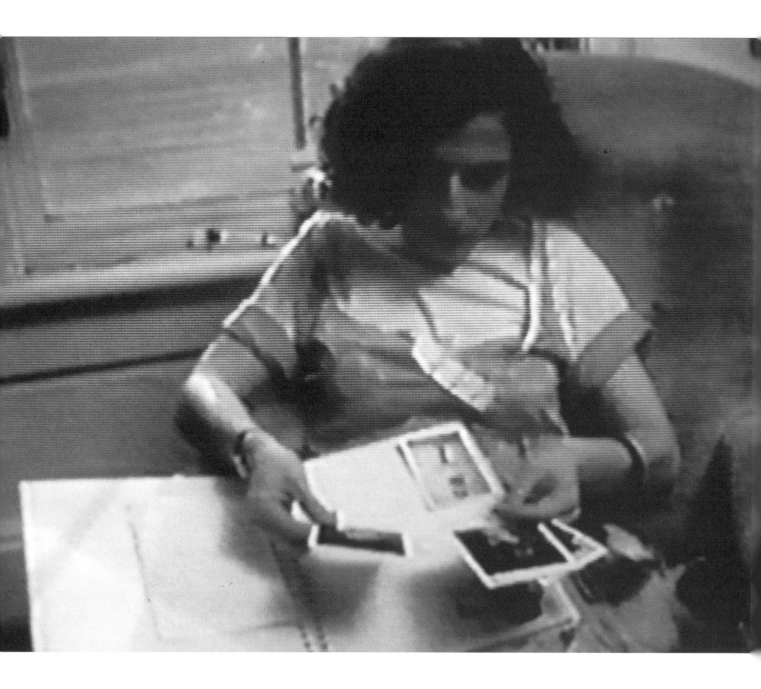

# NOTES

CONQUERING WHAT THEY TELL US IS "NATURAL"

1. Interview with Gérard Grugeau for the release of *Speaking Parts*, in *24 Images*.

2. In the volume edited by Sylvain Garel and André Pâquet, *Les cinéma du Canada*, published in 1992 for the major retrospective organized by the Georges Pompidou Center.

3. "La nouvelle vague ontarienne," in *Les cinéma du Canada*, op. cit. above, p. 147.

4. Ibid.

5. This procedure seems to interest Atom Egoyan, as he uses it elsewhere. To take only one example: in *Speaking Parts* the camera zooms in on a video image, framing the shot around an extra in the background. The recentering can't be logical in the film being watched on video; rather, it corresponds to an indication concerning the desire of the female character and her gaze on the male body.

6. Interview with Philippe Rouyer, published in the magazine *Positif*, December 1991.

7. *Images* (Paris: Gallimard, 1990), p. 62.

8. Since his very first short, Atom Egoyan's production company has been named "Ego Art Films."

9. Interview with Samuel Blumensfeld, published in the magazine *Les Inrockuptibles*, June 1993.

10. She burns images of Lebanon in an ashtray.

11. Interview published in the magazine *Positif*, December 1991.

THE PLACE OF THE SPECTATOR

1. "There is no more fantasizing in documentaries. The most elementary modesty forbids one from becoming the voyeur of intimate passions, vile desires, secret dramas. Fiction exists, to offer a field of expression free of all judgment, for better or worse.... Canadian cinema is not very physical, in all the senses of the word, beginning with desire. Nothing is more illuminating than the treatment accorded, not so much to the sins of the flesh, nor to obscenity and erotism, but to what happens on the level of bodies in a given society. There is no better barometer, since a culture serves above all to take on a certain number of tensions: and these tensions, the primary ones, the strongest ones, come out through the body." Gilles Carle, *Le cinéma canadien* (forthcoming).

2. Pasolini, *L'expérience hérétique*.

3. Dionysos, god of wine, son of Zeus and Semeledont, whose worship in Greece during theatrical representations is held to have been the origin of Tragedy (see Nietzsche, *The Birth of Tragedy*).

4. Hera (Arsinée Khanjian) must wear glasses when she watches films in her role as censor.

5. Mircea Eliade

6. Marcel Detienne *L'Invention de la mythologie*, Gallimard, 1981

7. Gaston Bachelard, *La Terre et la rêverie de la volonté* (Paris, Corti).

8. Interview between Atom Egoyan and Samuel Blumenfeld in *Les Inrockuptibles*, June, 1993.

9. The French word for "hearth," *foyer*, is related etymologically to the Latin *focus*, evoking the lens of the camera.

10. Nietzsche, *The Birth of Tragedy*.

11. Marcel Detienne *L'Invention de la mythologie*, Gallimard, 1981

12. Daniel Dobbels, in *Danses Tracées* (Paris, Dis Voir, 1991).

13. "It seems that man is born on an anvil like a chain, enchained vertebra by vertebra, riveted piece by piece. This first chain, this fundamental metallic being, is the serpent from which man will be made to grow. When the serpent grows, it is always by an intimate bursting, pushing the metal of its scales outside." Bachelard, *La Terre et la rêverie de la volonté*, p. 181.

14. "Psychological phenomenology has always cut between the signified noumenon and the signifying phenomenon, most often confusing the role of the mental image with the signs of language. In the symbol that constitutes the image, there is a homogeneity of signifier and signified within one organizing dynamism: thus the image differs totally from the arbitrary sign. This symbol does not fall into the domain of semiotics, but belongs to a special semantics." G. Durand, *Les Structures anthropologiques de l'imaginaire* (Paris, Bordas, 1969). This passage can be related to the notion of metaphor as found in numerous interviews with Egoyan.

15. Jean Louis Schaefer, in *L'homme ordinaire du cinéma* (Paris, Gallimard, 1980).

16. Jacqueline Lichtenstein, in *Art Press*, July-August, 1992.

17. Daniel Dobbels, op. cit.

18 Jacqueline Lichtenstein, op. cit.

19. Pasolini, op. cit.

20. In *Dictionnaire des Symboles* (Robert Laffont, 1982).

# PHOTO INDEX